PREPARING FOR
THE GREAT
Outpouring

PREPARING FOR
THE GREAT
Outpouring

CHARLES R. FOX, PHD

BRIDGE
LOGOS

Newberry, FL 32669

Bridge-Logos

Newberry, FL 32669

Preparing for the Great Outpouring:
Is Your Heart Ready for A Move of God?

by Charles R Fox, PhD.

Printed in the United States of America.

Library of Congress Catalog Card Number: 2020940391

International Standard Book Number: 978-1-61036-250-4

Cover/Interior design by Kent Jensen | knail.com

Dedication

I want to first give thanks to my Lord and Savior Jesus Christ. None of this would be possible without Him giving me the strength. I dedicate this book to my loving wife April and our children—Gabby and Isaiah. Love you family! You are my inspiration. Your prayers and sacrificial love made the difference. I also want to thank the following people: my dad, Charles R. Fox, Sr. (thank you dad for leading me to the Lord and being such a great man of faith), my mom, Vicky Fox (Mombo) Mccallister (thanks for your love and always believing in me) and my mentor, Jon Ruthven (I love you "Doc" and thanks for teaching me how to write)!

Endorsements

Dr. Charles Fox has laid out a warm and loving insight into the heart of God and His desire for a great spiritual renewal. The pattern of preparation for revival that Dr. Fox lays out shows an unusually keen grasp of both biblical theology and spiritual perception. This book could easily become a classic, along the lines of *My Utmost for His Highest* and *Streams in the Desert*, but focused on the greatest revival in human history that Fox believes is soon to manifest.

—**JON RUTHVEN**, PHD, PROFESSOR EMERITUS, REGENT UNIVERSITY
SCHOOL OF DIVINITY, AUTHOR, *ON THE CESSATION OF THE CHARISMATA*
AND *WHAT'S WRONG WITH PROTESTANT THEOLOGY.*

Revival is not accidental. Furthermore, revival is not entirely sovereign. Yes, the specifics and uniquenesses of each Holy Spirit outpouring throughout history are up to God's sovereign choosing, but I am assured—no, convinced—that it's possible to position yourself for a life-changing move of the Holy Spirit. Dr. Charles Fox offers both a Biblical and historical perspective of the non-negotiable factors that will position you for personal revival and prepare the church for corporate outpouring.

—**LARRY SPARKS**, MDIV., PUBLISHER, DESTINY IMAGE, HOST, THE
PROPHETIC EDGE, AUTHOR OF *BREAKTHROUGH FAITH*; CO-AUTHOR
OF *ACCESSING THE GREATER GLORY* AND *THE FIRE THAT NEVER SLEEPS*,
LARRYSPARKSMINISTRIES.COM

Why do revivals come, and better yet, what can we do to prepare? In *Preparing For The Great Outpouring*, my friend Charles Fox does what few authors have done, by equipping you with a God given plan. Charles Fox is one of the greatest historians of revival history, and by reading this book, you are being equipped by one of God's generals on this subject. Now more than ever, we need a massive outpouring of God's Spirit, and this book is written for such a time as this. Read this book, apply the principles and prepare yourself for an encounter with God that will change your life forever.

—**WILL FORD**, PROFESSOR, CHRIST FOR THE NATIONS INSTITUTE,
AUTHOR, *THE DREAM KING: HOW THE DREAM OF MARTIN LUTHER KING JR. IS
BEING FULFILLED TO HEAL RACISM IN AMERICA.*

Table of Contents

Foreword

We are living in exciting times! What an amazing time to be alive! Many of the prophets are trumpeting the message of revival that's coming. "The great harvest is upon us!"—they are saying (I being one of them).

When Jesus came to this world, many were expecting the next great thundering man of wealth and power to rebuild the kingdom and reestablish order; yet He came as a baby in the humblest of conditions. It perplexed many living in that day. "Could any good thing come out of Nazareth?"(John 1:46) It flipped their notion of what it truly meant to be a King.

When I think of the term "harvest," I think of my good friend's father who is a farmer. After his hard work, labor and months of investing, when it comes time for the harvest, it's all hands on deck. It takes everyone working hard together to pull it off. In that season, they get to reap what they have sewn. It's time for Jesus to reap everything that He endured on the cross. It's time for the great harvest of souls.

What will bring about this great revival and harvest? Some may think—well the next great evangelist. But I would argue, I think that God is pointing the finger at each one of us in this season. It's not by accident that you and I are alive in this time of history. Each one of us has a part to play in the timeline of God.

Rather than a platform, or glamorous ministry, Dr. Charles Fox points to six traits that he sees as essential for each one of us to walk in, to bring about this great revival—Brokenness, Hunger, Prayer, Persistence, Thankfulness and Courage.

Lord let these be the mark on our generation! May our hearts be prepared and ready—for YOU ARE COMING! The outpouring is upon us!

—Ana Werner
Founder of Ana Werner Ministries
President, Eagles Network
Author of *The Seer's Path, Seeing Behind the Veil,*
The Warrior's Dance, co-author of *Accessing the Greater Glory*
www.anawerner.org

Introduction

I believe that the Church's best days are ahead of her. Recently, many prophetic voices and respected church leaders have been prophesying that a world-wide revival is imminent. I have also been sensing that the Lord is up to something. As a pastor I have definitely noticed the intensity increasing in our times of worship as a congregation. I also believe that the Lord has placed a desire for revival in the hearts of many today. With so many things going on in our world right now, we need a genuine move of the Holy Spirit.

Although I agree with those who claim that revival is coming and that we need a move of God, I believe that our hearts must be prepared for a revival. Though the Holy Spirit has spoken to many in the Body of Christ about the Lord's intentions for revival for America and for the entire world for that matter, our hearts need to be prepared for a move of the Spirit. *Preparing for the Great Outpouring: Is Your Heart Ready for A Move of God?* is not a magic formula for revival but the chapters were written to address ways in which God prepares our hearts individually for a move of the Spirit. In the following chapters, I delve into six areas that serve as indicators that a heart is prepared for revival. Through personal experience and research, I have come to the conclusion that brokenness, hunger, prayer, persistence, thankfulness and courage are key heart ingredients to the move of God. These indicators have accompanied past moves of the Spirit and are prophetic signals that our hearts are ready for the end time outpouring that God wants to send to the world!

A Broken Heart

Anytime God wants to send a fresh wind upon you or do anything significant with you, there will be a season of brokenness that you go through. Have you ever prayed the prayer? "Lord, please use me for your glory." "I just want you to use me." Perhaps you have even said the following: "Jesus, I want to know you better." Getting to this point in our Christian walk is important because it means that we have now become pliable for the Master's use. The only thing about praying these types of prayers is that before the Lord can do anything substantial in our lives, He has to break us.

Brokenness in the Life of David

How does God go about breaking us? One way is to break us through trouble that comes in our lives. King David, who wrote seventy-three Psalms in the Book of Psalms, understood the concept of brokenness and trouble. In Psalm 34, David wrote the following: *"The LORD is near to those who have a broken heart, and saves such as have a contrite spirit."* (Psalm 34:18 NKJV) David was a brokenhearted man in this Psalm because he had already fled from Saul who was trying to kill him because of jealousy and due to the anointing on David's life. He also was leaving his good friend Jonathan, the son of Saul, who was practically a brother to him. David wept bitterly. In his desperation to get away from Saul, David fled to King Achish of the Philistines, an enemy of Israel. The men in Achish's service identified David as the one who had slain his ten thousands (1 Samuel 21:11). In fear of his life, David began to act like he was a crazy man and started to drool. This story is remarkable. David was a man who was anointed to be the next king of Israel. Yet, he was so afraid that he changed his behavior in the presence of the king of the Philistines just to survive. The soon to be king of Israel had a promise from the Lord but in his distress he took refuge in the enemy's fortress.

I can just imagine David as an adolescent being anointed by Samuel. He must have been so excited after being chosen by God to be the next king. Now, several years later, he is now having second thoughts about his reign as king coming to pass. Why is David going through all of this? He has already received God's promise and approval as Israel's next king. I believe the answer to this question is that David's heart needed to be prepared to rule. Through David's experiences, the Lord was also preparing him to write the wonderful things of the Spirit that he jotted down in the Psalms. Trials, troubles and tests are ways in which God prepares the soil of our hearts for things of the Spirit. Tribulations are a consistent theme throughout the Bible and in the life of the believer today.

Sin

Another way that God prepares our hearts for revival is through brokenness over our sin. Though we as believers never want to get to this point of brokenness in our Christian walk, the Holy Spirit will convict us of our disobedience, sexual immorality, pride and flat out rebellion against the Lord. Paul's letters to the Corinthian believers were written to call the Corinthian church to repent of sin. In 2 Corinthians 7:8-11 Paul actually commended the Corinthian believers for their godly repentance. Here is what he said:

> For even if I made you sorry with my letter, I do not regret it; though I did regret it. For I perceive that the same epistle made you sorry, though only for a while. Now I rejoice, not that you were made sorry, but that your sorrow led to repentance. For you were made sorry in a godly manner, that you might suffer loss from us in nothing. For godly sorrow produces repentance leading to salvation, not to be regretted; but the sorrow of the world produces death. For observe this very thing, that you sorrowed in a godly manner: what diligence it produced in you, what clearing of yourselves, what indignation, what fear, what vehement desire, what zeal, what vindication! In all things you proved yourselves to be clear in this matter.   (2 Corinthians 7:8–11 NKJV)

Although writing the previous letter to the Corinthian believers made Paul feel sorry about their grief over his rebuke, he rejoiced at what it produced in them. As already stated, their godly sorrow led to repentance but it also produced vexation, holiness and a passion for God. When we are truly broken over our sin and repent, the Lord cleanses us (1 John 1:9). This cleansing creates a zeal for righteousness and brings about personal renewal. King David's prayer of repentance in Psalm 51 over his adulterous relationship with Bathsheba is another great example of what true brokenness over sin can produce (2 Samuel 11:1:26; 2 Samuel 12:1-13).

> *Purge me with hyssop, and I shall be clean; wash me, and I shall be whiter than snow. Make me hear joy and gladness, that the bones You have broken may rejoice. Hide Your face from my sins, and blot out all my iniquities. Create in me a clean heart, O God, and renew a steadfast spirit within me. Do not cast me away from Your presence, and do not take Your Holy Spirit from me. Restore to me the joy of Your salvation, and uphold me by Your generous Spirit. Then I will teach transgressors Your ways, and sinners shall be converted to You.* (Psalm 51:7–13 NKJV)

David's petition to the Lord to revitalize his spirit has been echoed by many Christians who have fallen into sin over the years. Similar to the Corinthian believers, David's brokenness led to repentance and zeal. His passion for God even motivated him to teach transgressors the ways of the Lord leading to their conversion.

Although we pray that our brothers and sisters in the Body of Christ will not have to experience the pain of falling into sin, the brokenness that comes from a heart that is restored can make us realize our need for God and make us poor in spirit (Matthew 5:3). It is my belief that God is raising up people right now in the Body of Christ who have been written off because of their moral failures. These people are like David and have a heart after God. They are pastors, church leaders, politicians and people from every walk of life. If you are a believer reading this book and have struggled with some area of secret sin, you are the next person in line to be restored to wholeness. You may also be the next person that God uses to birth a move of the Holy Spirit in your region, country, city or sphere of influence.

Brokenness in the Life of Joseph

Joseph was a gifted young man who was favored by his father over his brothers. Jacob gave Joseph a multi-colored coat that further proved his father's favoritism for Joseph over his other siblings. God gave Joseph several dreams about future greatness.

> *"...Please hear this dream which I have dreamed: There we were, binding sheaves in the field. Then behold, my sheaf arose and also stood upright; and indeed your sheaves stood all around and bowed down to my sheaf. And his brothers said to him, "Shall you indeed reign over us? Or shall you indeed have dominion over us?" So they hated him even more for his dreams and for his words. Then he dreamed still another dream and told it to his brothers, and said, "Look, I have dreamed another dream. And this time, the sun, the moon, and the eleven stars bowed down to me."*
>
> (Genesis 37:6–9 NKJV)

Joseph's dreams did indeed come true but not the way he expected. Though God's plan was to use Joseph mightily, Joseph's heart had to be prepared. He was sold into slavery by his brothers and was sent to Egypt. He was later falsely accused of rape by Potiphar's wife and then thrown in prison.

I believe there are many Josephs in the Body of Christ today who have dreamed about their futures and have seen visions of themselves being in the center of the next move of God. These individuals are gifted and eager to fulfill their destinies. But, like Joseph, they need to be broken and walk through the crucible of character. The pain of betrayal by his brothers, his slavery and subsequent imprisonment prepared Joseph to be greatly used by God. In every circumstance, whether he was serving his master Potiphar, resisting temptation from the wife of Potiphar or serving the keeper of the jail to which he was confined, God gave him favor and Joseph grew because of his suffering (Genesis 37:23; 39:7-20; 39:21-23; 40:1-23).

Joseph's hardships in Egypt produced a humility that matched his giftedness, something that he clearly did not have before he was sold by his brothers. Joseph was able to combine humility and giftedness in leadership when he was elevated from prison to second in command in Egypt by Pharaoh (Genesis 41:1-37). Brokenness was also on display when Joseph's brothers came to Egypt to buy grain due to the famine that had reached Canaan (Genesis 42:1-3). His brothers came and bowed to him as God foretold Joseph in his dream. As they bowed, they did not recognize him but Joseph knew who they were. Joseph tested his brothers by accusing them of being spies. He confined them for three days and released everyone but Simeon, sending them back with grain for their families and requiring them to come back with their younger brother Benjamin (Genesis 42:6-20). Still unaware of Joseph's true identity, the brothers were vexed with guilt having sold their brother into slavery years before (Genesis 42:21-22). Having overheard their discussion, Joseph began to weep secretly (Genesis 42:23-24).

Due to the severity of the famine, Joseph's brothers had to make a return trip back to Egypt to buy more food. Joseph's younger brother Benjamin was included in their number this time because Joseph commanded that they bring him. After eating with his brothers and testing them once again, Joseph finally reveals his identity to his brothers and tells them not be angry with themselves because it was God that sent him to Egypt to preserve them (Genesis 45:1-3; Genesis 45:4-8).

I believe God wants to pour out His Spirit on a Joseph generation whose hearts are being prepared for revival by the crucible of character. Like Joseph, these individuals are being prepared to sustain nations and lead mighty moves of God. God is molding them into what He wants them to be so that they will bear fruit in due season.

A few years ago I was invited to speak at a chapel service at a Christian university. I was excited because they wanted me to come speak about one of my favorite topics—revival! The topic of revival was chosen by this university as a yearlong theme. There were many spiritually gifted young people in attendance. Although there were several people who were desperate for God and received a touch from the Lord that day during the ministry time, I began to discern that many hearts were not prepared for revival. They seemed to want revival on their own terms without having their hearts broken in the presence of the Lord. What I observed that day at this university is a microscopic prophetic picture of what is happening right now within the Body of Christ. Many see the need for revival and want to hear preaching or even prophecies about revival. Few, however, truly want to pay the price of brokenness for revival.

Staying Broken

How does a believer stay in a perpetual state of humility or brokenness? Sometimes it is easier to be contrite when we are going through trials, troubles or struggling with some area of sin in our lives. Many believers struggle, however, to remain broken before the Lord when they have all the money they need, are in good physical health or if they are in a season of overall prosperity. As I have preached on the subject of the importance of staying broken, I have found people really want to walk in a constant state of humility but just do not know how. The Lord Jesus Christ actually gave insight into this in Matthew's gospel in the beatitudes. *"Blessed are the poor in spirit, for theirs is the kingdom of heaven."* (Matthew 5:3 NKJV) What does it really mean to be poor in spirit? The New Living Translation Bible is helpful in this regard: *"God blesses those who are poor and realize their need for him, for the Kingdom of Heaven is theirs."* (Matthew 5:3 NLT) The secret to walking in a lifestyle of brokenness is to maintain a helpless dependence on the Lord.

William J. Seymour

William J. Seymour, leader of the Azusa Street Revival,[1] was a man who demonstrated a life of brokenness and dependency on the Holy Spirit. Azusa participant, William Durham, said this about Seymour:

> "He is the meekest man I ever met. He walks and talks with God. His power is in his weakness. He seems to maintain a helpless dependence on God and is simple-hearted as a little child, and at the same time is so filled with God that you feel the love and power every time you get near him."[2]

---

1   Vinson Synan and Charles R. Fox, Jr., *William J. Seymour: Pioneer of the Azusa Street Revival* (Alachua, FL: Bridge Logos, 2012), 11. Life Magazine and *USA Today* listed the Azusa Street Revival as one of the top hundred nation-impacting events of the Twentieth Century.

2   William H. Durham, "A Chicago Evangelist's Pentecost," *The Apostolic Faith* 1, no. 6 (February to March 1907): 4.

Though thousands of people came through the doors of the Azusa Street Mission to be touched by the Holy Spirit, Seymour stayed humble, admonishing participants to keep their focus on the Lord. Seymour never lost his focus because of the success of the revival as people traveled from all over the world to receive the baptism of the Holy Spirit. What allowed Seymour to maintain his brokenness was his prayer life. Azusa Street chronicler and participant Frank Bartleman reported that Seymour was so humble that he would often be seen at the revival praying with his head in one of the two empty crates which held shoeboxes that he used as a makeshift pulpit.[3]

John and Carol Arnott

John and Carol Arnott, who were senior pastors of the Toronto Airport Vineyard Church (birthplace of what is known as the Toronto Blessing Outpouring), are great examples of how the Holy Spirit uses brokenness in the lives of His servants to spark revival. Before coming together to wed in 1979, both went through the tragedy of divorce and disappointment.

Shortly after attending Ontario Bible College in Toronto from 1966 to 1969, John Arnott experienced the end to his first marriage, citing irreconcilable differences. Feeling like a failure and going through depression, John stated, "I ended up with my two daughters kind of looking after dad."[4]

After making a vow to himself that he would never allow another woman to hurt him like his first wife ever again, Carol

3 Frank Bartleman, *Azusa Street* (South Plainfield, NJ: Bridge Publishing, 1980), 58.

4 Jerry Steingard and John Arnott, *From Here to the Nations: The Story of the Toronto Blessing* (Toronto ON, Canada: Catch the Fire Books, 2014), Kindle Edition, Loc 730.

Sandra Bechtold (who would later become Carol Arnott) became instrumental in breaking down the defenses that surrounded John's heart as the two wed in 1979.[5]

Carol also suffered tremendous brokenness in her first marriage as well due to her husband and high school sweetheart leaving her for a younger woman. The Lord healed Carol of her broken heart by revealing himself to her in the midst of her pain.

After returning from a short term missions trip in Indonesia the following year after their wedding, John and Carol Arnott began to sense a strong calling for full time pastoral ministry. Though the couple struggled with feeling like they were disqualified because of their previous marriages ending in divorce, the Lord made it clear to them that they were to start a church in Carol's hometown of Stratford. After obeying the voice of God to leave their business behind for ministry, the Arnotts humbly yielded themselves to the Lord by saying, "Lord, we're just a couple of broken pieces; if you can use us to build your Kingdom, that would be great."[6]

Frank Damazio comments on the importance of brokenness in his book, Seasons of Revival:

> "Anything that is broken is deemed by man to be unfit, and he ends up throwing it away. But to God, only that which is broken is useful. Just as flowers yield their perfume when they are crushed and grapes produce wine when they are squashed, so the vessels of God—His people—are ready for revival only when they are broken. God's vessels, the ones He uses, are broken vessels."[7]

---

5   Ibid., Loc 732.
6   Ibid., Loc 753.
7   Ibid. Loc 758.

The Lord certainly used these broken people to spearhead one of the greatest revivals in North American Church history when revival broke out at Toronto Airport Vineyard on January 20, 1994 while visiting pastor Randy Clark was sharing his testimony.

Randy Clark

When Randy Clark was asked by Pastor John Arnott to come to Toronto for a four-day meeting, Clark could never have fathomed that this little meeting would have worldwide implications. Randy did not realize that God would take this former Baptist pastor and use him to not only spread revival fire in Toronto but to the rest of the world. Randy Clark, however, had to go through a breaking process.

As a young preacher with tremendous passion to preach the Word of God, Randy Clark got married at the tender age of nineteen.[8] Randy, who was from a small town in southern Illinois, was married in July 1971 to a young woman trying to escape an abusive home. His wife's dysfunction manifested very early in the marriage, even during their honeymoon. Though Randy would go through two years of counseling to try and save his marriage, the relationship was basically over when the couple separated after three volatile years. As a seminary student at this time, Randy began to have other problems in his life as he came under the influence of liberal theology.

Clark had become so theologically liberal by sitting under the teaching of one of his professors that he even started disbelieving that there was a real devil or demons.[9] Dr. Smith, who was one

---

8   Randy Clark, *Lighting Fires*, (Apostolic Network of Global Awakening, 2011), Kindle edition Loc, 547.

9   Ibid., Loc, 583.

of Randy's favorite professors, said the following concerning Randy's newfound liberalism, "Randy, do you know your views are changing? If you go back to southern Illinois now, you're going to be hurt by the church. Do you love the church enough to serve it . . . even when it hurts?"[10] Though Randy would respond to his mentor by saying that he was willing to serve the church even if it meant he would suffer, it was not long before he discovered the price for serving the church.

During Randy's separation, he learned from a reliable source that his wife was having an affair. The news about his wife's infidelity ended Randy's hopes for his marriage and the couple decided to proceed with the divorce. The consequences of the divorce proceedings began to affect Randy adversely, especially as it pertained to his denomination. Divorced men were not allowed to minister.

Before the divorce proceedings, Randy was being groomed to become the pastor of one of the larger Baptist churches in his city. He had already registered to attend Southern Baptist Theological Seminary in Louisville, Kentucky. With the impending end to his marriage, however, all of Randy's plans for ministry were now up in the air. Randy explained how his marriage situation began to affect him at seminary.

> During my first year there, all the students were given the Minnesota Multiphasic Personality Inventory, which consisted of about five hundred questions. When my results came in, the Dean of Students invited me to his office to discuss them: "We have some problems here, Clark," he said, with a serious look on his face. "Some of these answers

---

10 Ibid., Loc, 589.

you gave just don't seem to fit together. For example, this test shows that you should be on the verge of a nervous breakdown, but you're not. How do you explain this?"[11]

As Randy Clark began to tell the Dean of Students the kind of turmoil he had been through and that his divorce would be final in a few weeks, visibly disturbed, the Dean responded—"Divorce? What divorce?"[12]

Randy was under the impression that those who were divorced could still attend Southern Baptist Theological Seminary. Unfortunately for him, the Dean told him that he had received wrong information about the seminary's position on divorce. Only men who were divorced and remarried could actually attend. Randy would have to leave the seminary because he would be divorced and not remarried. Randy shared some of the last few painful words of advice from the Dean before he left seminary: "You're a bright student; enter law school. Don't come back...You'll never have a ministry."[13]

Having been divorced and kicked out of seminary, Randy Clark was a broken man. He had a major decision to make. Would he spend the rest of his life blaming God over lost dreams or would he accept the advice of his mentor Dr. Smith to "love the church enough to serve it when it hurts?" After dealing with inner turmoil, Randy would submit to God by loving the church in the midst of his pain. The Lord would not only restore Randy to ministry but He would give him a second chance at love by bringing DeAnne Davenport into his life. The two were married on July 12th 1975 and are still best friends today. The man who

11 Ibid., Loc 610.
12 Ibid., Loc 614.
13 Ibid., Loc 632.

was told that he would never have a ministry has a ministry that spreads renewal all over the world, impacting thousands of people.

If we as believers want to experience the outpouring of the Holy Spirit, we must stay in a place of brokenness. The place of brokenness is at the foot of the cross. We must keep our eyes on Jesus. He is the one that has taken our sin and has nailed it to His cross (Colossians 2:14). Though trials, trouble, persecution, suffering and sin in our lives are ways in which the Lord humbles us, we stay broken by constantly beholding the face of our Lord Jesus Christ. When we stay in the presence of God through prayer and waiting on the Lord, we are acknowledging our need for Him and are able to remain broken and poor in spirit.

2

A Hungry Heart

As the deer pants for the water brooks, so pants my soul for You,
O God. My soul thirsts for God, for the living God. When shall I
come and appear before God? (Psalm 42:1-2 NKJV)

Having been in ministry for over twenty-five years and studying outpourings of the Holy Spirit, I have discovered a common denominator present in every person who experienced revival—hunger! In the Psalm above, the psalmist expresses hunger for God in a wonderful word picture using a deer's desire for water. Most seasoned deer hunters understand the habits of deer. Mature deer normally bed close to a water source, within seventy-five feet. Studies show that deer drink between three to five quarts of water a day. Because of a deer's propensity to drink, hunters can take advantage by setting up shop next to water. It is ironic that a deer's close proximity to the water is a source of sustenance but can also be the reason for its demise. What is so awesome about the Christian life is that staying close to our water source gives us nothing but life. As we spend time in the presence of God, we stay connected to our source of life and develop more of an appetite for the things of God.

Several years ago I was preaching at our church on the subject of spiritual hunger. As I was speaking, I illustrated the message by telling the congregation to imagine a banquet table of delicious food prepared for you by God himself. The Lord has prepared our favorite recipes and desserts but the sad thing is that we cannot partake of this wonderful feast because we do not have an appetite. When I was an adolescent, I would hear from most of the adults that eating sweets like ice cream and cake close to dinner time would ruin my appetite. It did not ruin it so much as it did give more of a craving for sweets than eating a healthy dinner. One of the reasons why believers struggle with spiritual hunger is that they have built up an appetite for other things.

In many churches, authentic Spirit-led worship has been replaced by entertainment. Believers are at times critical of worship that centers more on God than themselves. The people who think this way would say that what I am saying about them is absolutely not true. I have been in enough places, however, to negate their opinions on this matter. There are many churches that try to create a concert atmosphere every Sunday with songs that only focus on the individuals sitting in the seats. I began to label this as "me worship." Oftentimes, the focus never really gets the attention on how great God is or how much He has done for us. It centers on what is popular in contemporary Christian music. This is not to say that I do not like some of the music or that I do not listen to it at times. If a ministry never really sings songs that accentuate the attributes of God or focuses on the Lord Jesus, they will be left with a culture of shallowness. This will also affect their appetites for sincere worship. It will also make them self-centered instead of God-centered.

We not only need to develop a hunger for authentic worship over entertainment but the Body of Christ must make sure we are not replacing the anointing for charisma. We live in a day where many people are starting ministries not because they have been anointed, appointed or called by God. These people are going into ministry because they have the charisma to lead but they have little spiritual substance. They see church planting as some sort of business startup that will turn into a cash cow. The sad thing is that many believers have developed an appetite for these charismatic individuals. Those who buy into their hype have lost the ability to discern between the anointing and charisma. They struggle to receive ministry from those who are not flamboyant like the television preachers they support financially. In my life I developed more of a hunger for God by listening to anointed men and women of God. Their hunger for the Lord coupled with their brokenness made me want to experience God more. I wanted what they had and as I sought the Lord, I began to receive some of the same gifts and mantles of these wonderful saints.

Cultivating Hunger

When we align ourselves with other hungry people, it cultivates and increases our spiritual hunger. As I mentioned above, the Lord has blessed me countless times by reading, listening to or being in the presence of awesome men and women of God. Their hunger for God impacted my life and continues to do so. Twenty-six years ago, I had a wonderful baptism of the Holy Spirit where I began speaking in tongues. Before I had this experience,

I frequently watched a Spirit-filled evangelist on television named Morris Cerullo. As I read his material and watched his television program, I started developing more hunger for God. The desire for more of the Holy Spirit began to get so strong in me that I decided to fly to a conference that he was having in Orlando, Florida. The background surrounding that trip to Orlando, however, was not without its challenges.

I was going through a tough transition in my life at the time. I was in the military on convalescent leave. I had just received an unfavorable decision from a medical board hearing. I had a medical condition that attacked my kidneys and the board recommended that I be honorably discharged without any benefits because they claimed that I became sick before I went into the Army. I decided to appeal the decision from our home in South Carolina. I was only in my early twenties and living with my parents at the time. Due to the fact that I was still getting paid by the military at this time, I was able to purchase my plane ticket and pay the registration for the conference. But I needed to pay for my hotel stay there and food. I had budgeted correctly for the trip. I was depending on my military paycheck for the rest of the expenses. As I was preparing for the conference and anticipating my paycheck, I received notification from the military that I had lost my appeal and was officially honorably discharged from the military. I was stunned because I really believed that I would win the appeal. I even had a dream before the decision that I believed to be from the Holy Spirit that I won and received a one hundred percent rating.

I had a problem. My trip was now in jeopardy. I was not going to receive the paycheck I was counting on to finish paying for the trip. I began to pray and ask the Lord what to do. I knew

I could not put the "bite" on my parents for the money because they had other responsibilities. It was now the day before the conference and the plane was due to leave in the morning. I was considering canceling the trip but there was one thing that kept me from postponing it—hunger. I wanted more of God and could not give up. It was three o'clock in the morning when I began packing. My faith got to the point that I actually believed that the Lord was going to have someone at the airport give me the rest of the money for conference costs.

It was late morning when my parents and I set out for the airport in Fayetteville, North Carolina. When we arrived at the airport, my father gave me a little over two hundred dollars. I was stunned because I knew it was a sacrifice for him, especially with everything else he had to pay that month to keep the household afloat. Although the money he gave was still not enough to pay for my hotel costs, I felt extremely blessed to have a dad who was walking by faith with me and planted a seed for my spiritual growth. He understood my desire for more of God and I am still grateful for his love. His surprising seed gift gave me even more confidence that the Lord would provide everything I needed during my stay in Florida for the conference. The Lord did far above all I could possibly conceive. My life was forever changed at this conference. I received what I desired. I was baptized in the Holy Spirit and felt the Lord's tangible presence throughout my stay. On the last day of the conference, I was down to my last twenty dollars. It was Friday and I knew I had to check out of my room after the morning session was over. The problem was that my plane did not leave until Sunday morning. I was supposed to stay in the hotel until Sunday and get a cab to the airport but did not have enough money. During the morning offering, the

Holy Spirit began to speak to me. "Give the twenty dollars in the offering." At that time, I did not believe it was the Holy Spirit. Why would God tell me to give my last dollars? I reasoned. I was really struggling with this. Then the Lord began to reason back at me. "Twenty dollars will not be enough for you to stay in the hotel for two more nights. Trust me." I also needed to eat for two more days. Reluctantly, I gave the money in the offering. After the morning session, I went back to my hotel room and laid prostrate before the Lord. "What do you want me to do?" While in prayer, I sensed the Lord telling me to go back over to the conference hall.

When I arrived back at the conference hall, many people were still there basking in the glory of God's presence and fellowshipping with one another. I sat down in a chair in the back of the room and noticed a young man probably in his late twenties to my right. He actually looked like the actor Mel Gibson. I had seen this man several times during the conference but I never really spoke to him. We had only exchanged pleasantries. Then I began to hear the Holy Spirit say, "Ask him." I knew exactly what the Holy Spirit wanted me to ask. He wanted me to ask this man, who I did not know, if I could stay with him a few days until I could catch my flight on Sunday. As I think about what happened next, even twenty-six years later, I am still amazed at what the Lord did in my situation. After I formally introduced myself and told him my story, he smiled. He told me to wait in the back of the conference room because he wanted to talk it over with his younger brother who lived with him. I was elated when he came and informed me that it was okay with them for me to stay a few days at their residence.

When I arrived at their house, I was amazed at how nice their home was. I was blown away when they shared their testimony with me. These young men had just gone through a radical transformation in their lives. They were ex-drug dealers who received Christ shortly before the conference. These two brothers were now on fire for God. We had a wonderful two days of fellowship. We barbecued and even went to singles night at Benny Hinn's church on Saturday night and also attended the Sunday morning service. After the Sunday service, they drove me to the airport and we said our goodbyes. My life was forever changed because I saw the Lord provide for me supernaturally and use these two former drug dealers to take care of me. I included this story in this book because it illustrates how important hunger is to spiritual renewal. Without spiritual hunger, I would never have made the trip. I would have missed out on all the wonderful things God had in store for me. This conference became the springboard for my life and ministry.

As I mentioned previously, sometimes the Lord will use people and things to cultivate hunger within us. My wife and I are avid movie watchers. Her background is in theater and communications. I love to watch Rocky movies. One of my favorite Rocky flicks is Rocky III. In the movie, actor Sylvester Stallone (Rocky) has achieved success as the heavyweight champion of the world by defending his title multiple times. He has become wealthy and comfortable with who he has become. The main problem is that he has lost the hunger that made him rise to prominence. Rocky loses his title to a man by the name of Clubber Lang (Mr. T) who was hungry and desperate for Rocky's title. Rocky later teams up with former champion Apollo Creed

(Carl Weathers, who he defeated to become champion) for the purpose of reclaiming his heavyweight championship belt.

As Rocky trains with Apollo for the rematch, it becomes clear that Rocky is going through the motions and is a mere shadow of himself. He finally acknowledges to his wife that he is afraid. I love this movie because it reminds me of how the Lord restores our passion for Him. In order for Sylvester Stallone's character Rocky to get his hunger back, he needs to come to the realization that he is afraid and no longer passionate about boxing. Similarly, we as believers must first acknowledge when we have lost our hunger for the Lord in order to start the process of restoration. Rocky's training had a turnaround after his confession to his wife. He spent more time in the gym to regain "the eye of the tiger," a major theme of the movie. This phrase was repeated many times in the movie to imply passion and hunger for boxers. God prepares our hearts for a move of the Holy Spirit by taking us back to our "spiritual gyms." To use a real boxing example, when asked how he was able to knock down Muhammad Ali in round fifteen to win what was labeled as "The Fight of the Century", heavyweight champion Joe Frazier told the media "that he had go back to the gym" to land a crushing left hook to Ali's jaw. Like Frazier, the spiritual gym for the believer is the place where we first developed our passion for the Lord. It is a place of instruction, blood, sweat and tears. The spiritual gym for the believer is where we first encountered the Lord in a powerful way.

Bonafide spiritual encounters with God are essential for the life of the believer. They make us hungry for more of God and make us want to pursue Him. Due to certain denominational doctrines, fear and religiosity, some believers struggle with the supernatural. Even though there are counterfeit supernatural experiences from the enemy, believers must realize that the God of the Bible is a supernatural God who wants to encounter His people in a variety of ways such as dreams, visions, angelic visitations or through a personal appearance from the Lord Jesus. These examples are all biblical and these occurrences are happening today more and more as the return of the Lord gets closer. Though the Apostle Paul had several supernatural encounters that were mentioned in Scripture, there is one that really stands out that I believe became his spiritual gym and point of reference in his ministry. Luke recorded Paul's retelling of his conversion encounter as he stood before King Agrippa in Acts.

> *"While thus occupied, as I journeyed to Damascus with authority and commission from the chief priests, at midday, O king, along the road I saw a light from heaven, brighter than the sun, shining around me and those who journeyed with me. And when we all had fallen to the ground, I heard a voice speaking to me and saying in the Hebrew language, 'Saul, Saul, why are you persecuting Me? It is hard for you to kick against the goads.' So I said, 'Who are You, Lord?' And He said, 'I am Jesus, whom you are persecuting. But rise and stand on your feet; for I have appeared to you for this purpose, to make you a minister and a witness both of the things which you have seen and of the things which I will yet reveal to you. I will deliver you from the Jewish people, as well as from the Gentiles, to whom I now send you, to open their eyes, in order to turn them from darkness to light, and from the power of Satan to God, that they may receive forgiveness of sins and an inheritance among those who are sanctified by faith in Me.' "Therefore, King Agrippa, I was not disobedient to the heavenly vision, but declared first to those in Damascus and in Jerusalem, and throughout all*

the region of Judea, and then to the Gentiles, that they should repent, turn to God, and do works befitting repentance..."

(Acts 26:12–20 NKJV)

Paul's encounter with the Lord Jesus on the way to Damascus not only defined his ministry but it gave him an insatiable hunger that enabled him to walk through beatings, abandonment, conflicts, imprisonment and to stare in the face of death when he was stoned by the Jews. This one encounter kept him focused and he frequently shared his testimony as he ministered. One encounter with the Lord can change everything. Personally, I have had many wonderful heavenly encounters but similar to Paul, there is one that keeps me hungry for God and has defined my ministry. Even now as I write this chapter, emotions flood my soul because of the experience.

It is doubtless not profitable for me to boast. I will come to visions and revelations of the Lord: I know a man in Christ who fourteen years ago—whether in the body I do not know, or whether out of the body I do not know, God knows—such a one was caught up to the third heaven. And I know such a man—whether in the body or out of the body I do not know, God knows—how he was caught up into Paradise and heard inexpressible words, which it is not lawful for a man to utter. (2 Corinthians 12:1–4 NKJV)

Almost twenty-six years ago, I had an encounter with my Lord and Savior Jesus Christ. Like Paul, I did not know if I was in the body or out of my body. The Lord only knows. What I do know is that the encounter left me with an insatiable hunger for more of God. At the time of the encounter, I was spending several hours a day in presence of the Lord. During this time, the

Lord began to build a desire in me to preach the gospel all over the world. I had been asking the Lord to open doors for me to minister. Although I had just been newly baptized in the Holy Spirit, I was attending a small church in South Carolina where the gifts of the Holy Spirit were not really encouraged by the pastor but not prohibited. An evangelist visited our fellowship and confirmed through prophecy that the Lord was calling me to ministry and basically said everything that I was speaking to the Lord in my prayer closet. It was not long after the visit that I had a vision of being in heaven and saw Jesus. I was lying down on an altar. As I looked up, I saw the Lord smiling at me. Then, what He did next would change my life forever. He began to toss down over His shoulder what appeared to be fireballs. These fireballs went right into the middle of my chest. They felt wonderful. I never felt so much power and energy. I knew that they were going to the very core of my being. He continued to smile with every toss. He then stopped when He got to the number seven. I did not want it to end. I never felt more alive. It was sheer ecstasy. After the last fireball from Jesus I was instantly back at my parents' house in McColl, South Carolina.

Though I did not have full understanding at the time of the encounter with the Lord, this experience set me on a quest to know Him. The Holy Spirit revealed the meaning of the vision over twenty years later. The Lord directed me to the fourth chapter of Revelation:

> *And from the throne proceeded lightnings, thunderings, and voices. Seven lamps of fire were burning before the throne, which are the seven Spirits of God.* (Revelation 4:5 NKJV)

Most Bible scholars and theologians agree that the seven Spirits of God refer to the Holy Spirit. The Lord showed me that the seven fireballs represented the fullness of the Holy Spirit. Seven is a number of fullness or completion. Because Jesus was the one tossing down the seven fireballs and He is the baptizer in the Holy Spirit, this symbolized Him baptizing me with the Holy Spirit and fire (John 1:33). Glory to God! Although I am thankful and value every supernatural encounter the Lord gives me, I always go back to this one when times get tough. I remember that the Lord has given me the precious gift of the Holy Spirit and that much has been entrusted to me. This encounter has become my spiritual gym.

Last but certainly not least, we can cultivate spiritual hunger by feasting on the Word of God. We gain perspective on the primacy of the Word from the temptation of Jesus by Satan in the wilderness.

> *Then Jesus was led up by the Spirit into the wilderness to be tempted by the devil. And when He had fasted forty days and forty nights, afterward He was hungry. Now when the tempter came to Him, he said, "If You are the Son of God, command that these stones become bread. "But He answered and said, "It is written, 'Man shall not live by bread alone, but by every word that proceeds from the mouth of God.'"* (Matthew 4:1–4 NKJV)

Our Lord gave us an important key to maintaining our hunger for Him—unwavering dependence on the Word of God. I have preached that the more we eat the Word, the hungrier we get for the Word. We maintain natural hunger for food by consistently eating. Our natural appetite for food begins to diminish if we do not eat. Many believers claim that the Bible is the Word of God but only read it once a week. If they decided to eat natural food just on Sundays, they would become weak and struggle with malnutrition. How many Christians suffer from spiritual malnutrition because they only open their Bibles on Sunday mornings? Desire to read the Word of God serves as a litmus test that our hearts are ready for revival. Reading the Bible gives us the desire to encounter the God of the Bible.

Scripture also helps us not to get into error and assists us in determining if supernatural experiences are truly from God. How would we know to test the spirits to discern a genuine move of God if we do not know that the Bible actually warns us to test them? 1 John 4:1-3 states the following:

> *Beloved, do not believe every spirit, but test the spirits, whether they are of God; because many false prophets have gone out into the world. By this you know the Spirit of God: Every spirit that confesses that Jesus Christ has come in the flesh is of God, and every spirit that does not confess that Jesus Christ has come in the flesh is not of God. And this is the spirit of the Antichrist, which you have heard was coming, and is now already in the world.*
>
> (1 John 4:1–3 NKJV)

The day of Pentecost, described by Luke in the Book of Acts, is a great example of how Peter uses Scripture to confirm and explain the coming of the Holy Spirit.

> *But Peter, standing up with the eleven, raised his voice and said to them, "Men of Judea and all who dwell in Jerusalem, let this be known to you, and heed my words. For these are not drunk, as you suppose, since it is only the third hour of the day. But this is what was spoken by the prophet Joel: 'And it shall come to pass in the last days, says God, that I will pour out of My Spirit on all*

flesh; Your sons and your daughters shall prophesy, Your young men shall see visions, Your old men shall dream dreams. And on My menservants and on My maidservants I will pour out My Spirit in those days; And they shall prophesy. I will show wonders in heaven above and signs in the earth beneath: Blood and fire and vapor of smoke. The sun shall be turned into darkness, and the moon into blood, before the coming of the great and awesome day of the Lord. And it shall come to pass That whoever calls on the name of the Lord Shall be saved.' (Acts 2:14–21 NKJV)

In the passage above Peter quotes the prophet Joel to clarify to international Jews and mockers in Jerusalem why he and the other followers were speaking in tongues. Peter basically uses Joel 2:28-32 like a proof text in explaining the mighty outpouring of the Holy Spirit. This is an example that we who love revival must emulate. I believe that God is preparing our hearts for the greatest outpouring the earth has ever seen but in the midst of this coming move of the Spirit, the enemy will send counterfeits to try to deceive the people of God. Believers will not be misled if they stay rooted in the Word of God and test the spirits.

If we are to stay hungry for God, it is important we associate with individuals and ministries that are deeply in love with the Lord and hungry for more of His presence. I am always blessed when I listen to individuals greatly used of God like Bill Johnson, senior leader of Bethel Church in Redding, California or Randy Clark of Global Awakening. These two men have had tremendous supernatural encounters with God and have been used greatly in signs, wonders, miracles and healings. Yet both men have testified about traveling thousands of miles to receive impartations from other anointed people of God.

Though God encounters His children on a daily basis through a number of ways such as prayer and feasting on His Word, we must understand that there are times when God's manifest presence comes and transforms us to the point where we are never the same. These experiences increase our hunger for the Lord and make our hearts desperate to pursue Him for revival. People who are hungry increase their prayer time with the Lord which then leads to a prayerful heart.

3

A Prayerful Heart

Some people pray just to pray and some people pray to know God.   —Andrew Murray

Though we can list a number of reasons why prayer is important to the life of the believer, intimately knowing the Lord should be our primary motivation for spending time with God. In the previous chapter we talked about the importance of hunger in preparing our hearts for a move of the Spirit. Hunger is also essential to having an effective prayer life. Prayer and hunger should go hand and hand but many times that is not the case. It is possible to go through the rudimentary elements of prayer and not be hungry or genuinely sincere for God. Jesus accused the Pharisees of doing just that in the sixth chapter of Matthew's gospel.

> *"And when you pray, you shall not be like the hypocrites. For they love to pray standing in the synagogues and on the corners of the streets, that they may be seen by men. Assuredly, I say to you, they*

*have their reward. But you, when you pray, go into your room,
and when you have shut your door, pray to your Father who is in
the secret place; and your Father who sees in secret will reward
you openly."* (Matthew 6:5–6 NKJV)

Many years ago when I was a young traveling evangelist still
in my early twenties, I adopted a saying from a seasoned pastor
that has stayed with me till this day. The pastor would always
say, "Don't try to be a public success when you are really a private
failure." The Pharisees were private failures because they wanted
to get the attention and glory for their eloquent prayers in public
settings but their hearts were not right with God.

Like the Pharisees, some church leaders seem to always find
their way in front of the camera when it comes to prayer. They
have adopted a prayer life in public that is more nuanced and
eloquent to suit a politically correct charged climate. Why bring
up church leaders at this point? I believe the lack of emphasis on
prayer from pastors is one of the reasons the glory of God does
not fall in our churches. As a pastor, I must share some of the
blame. There have been times when I have been disappointed and
discouraged with the lack of attendance when it comes to prayer
meetings. There is a temptation to focus too much on programs
and other events that people will more readily attend. We must
not let this happen. If pastors and spiritual leaders spend enough
time in the presence of God, their congregations will know it.
The people they are leading will ask what the disciples requested
of Jesus. "Teach us how to pray..." (Luke 11:1) It is interesting
to note that the disciples did not ask Jesus how to preach. Jesus
not only encouraged them to pray but He modeled prayer to
His disciples. It was a lifestyle. I believe the disciples asked

Jesus to teach them to pray because they saw what His intimate relationship with His Father was producing. They observed that Jesus' prayer life was the source of the miracles, signs, wonders, exorcisms and even His public ministry of preaching.

An important part of being a ministry leader is equipping the saints for the work of the ministry and building up the believer (Ephesians 4:11). We as church leaders must realize, however, that modeling a lifestyle to those that we are equipping is essential to having an effective discipleship ministry.

For a number of years, I taught homiletics as a professor in seminary. As I began teaching men and women of God the art of preaching and sermon preparation, I adopted an incarnational method of teaching homiletics to my students from a friend and colleague of mine. Incarnational preaching comes from the word incarnation, which is the doctrine that Jesus as God the Son, or the Word, took on a human body by being conceived by the Holy Spirit in the womb of Mary. *And the Word became flesh and dwelt among us, and we beheld His glory, the glory as of the only begotten of the Father, full of grace and truth.* (John 1:14 NKJV)

Similar to the incarnation, incarnational preaching teaches that for a sermon to be effective, the communicator most clothe themselves in flesh. During the delivery of the sermon, the skeleton of the outline must take on the *"flesh"* of the person delivering the message. In observing my students, I was always checking to see if the person preaching was event focused or could I discern a lifestyle? Was the student just focused on completing an assignment or did their sermon display evidence of a genuine relationship with the Lord in their communication? Were they transparent with the audience by using personal illustrations? Could the hearers discern that the student had been with the

Lord? We see a wonderful example of the importance of lifestyle communication in the Book of Acts.

> *Now when they saw the boldness of Peter and John, and perceived that they were uneducated and untrained men, they marveled. And they realized that they had been with Jesus.*
>
> (Acts 4:13 NKJV)

In the example above, Peter and John were speaking boldly to the rulers and elders of Israel, having been arrested a day before. They were articulating their faith with such elegance, clarity and authority that it became obvious to the Jews that these men had spent significant time with Jesus. It did not matter how uneducated or how unqualified Peter and John were in the eyes of other people. What mattered most was that these men had been totally transformed in the presence of Jesus.

My dad, Charles R. Fox, Sr. has been an inspiration to me through the years. I would not be a Christian today if I had not spent most of my years drinking from his cup of wisdom. When I was a young traveling evangelist, he told me that without spending time in the presence of God I had nothing to give the people I was ministering to. What my father said has stayed with me until this present day. We live in an information age where there is a temptation for many preachers to reconstruct sermons taken from the internet instead of spending time in prayer to hear from the very heart of God.

Recently, I was reading an article entitled, "The Beginning of the Argentine Revival," based on the book, *The Secrets of the Argentine Revival* by R. Edward Miller. The article describes the desperation of a missionary who had been unsuccessful in his attempts to spread the gospel during his time in Argentina. The missionary pastored a small church in the city of Mendoza in Argentina in the year 1949 but his heart was to share the gospel in a neighboring town named Lavalle. The town of Lavalle was appealing to him because the gospel had never been preached there. After evaluating his missionary career at the time, the missionary came to the conclusion that his time in Argentina was a total failure.

The missionary was a broken man as he acknowledged that all of his efforts to succeed as a missionary had been fruitless. He even contemplated heading back to his country to get a job because he doubted the call to be a missionary. The missionary did not understand, however, that God would use his brokenness to prepare the soil of the man's heart for an outpouring of the Holy Spirit.

The Holy Spirit led the pastor to start praying eight hours a day. His missionary colleagues criticized him for spending so much time in prayer. They believed that no person who spent most of their time in prayer, "and not in the traditional missionary activities, had a right to receive a missionary's pay."[14]

In spite of the disapproval of his colleagues, the missionary made a decision to obey God rather than succumb to peer pressure. He was determined to seek the Lord in prayer and Bible reading. The man was determined to find answers for revival in Argentina. This missionary had something that I believe the Lord gives every person who is about to experience a personal outpouring—perseverance. Though we will speak more about persistence later, I will say a few a words about it now.

---

14 Evan Wiggs, "The Beginning of the Great Argentine Revival: Or the Rap on the Table that Started the Revival," accessed June 20, 2019, http://www.evanwiggs.com/revival/history/The%20Beginning%20 of%20the%20Great%20Argentine%20Revival.htm

A major way the Lord prepares us for a move of His Spirit is to stir our hearts to persevere through whatever barrier is hindering our supernatural breakthrough to encountering the manifest presence of God. In this missionary's situation, the hindrance he had to push through happened to be the very people who were supposed to be supporting him—his missionary colleagues. This pastor and missionary had to be bold enough to persevere by breaking tradition as it pertained to the culture that his fellow missionaries wholeheartedly embraced.

The other missionaries criticized the man for "stepping out of the box" by spending most of his time in prayer instead of being concerned with best practices for missionaries. Jesus describes the importance of perseverance when speaking about the kingdom of God.

> And from the days of John the Baptist until now the kingdom of heaven suffers violence, and the violent take it by force.
> (Matthew 11:12 NKJV)

Seeking God requires us to press into Him. Apprehending the Lord is comparable to fishing. When I was a child, I used to love to go fishing with my dad. We lived close to the beach in Rockaway Beach, Queens, New York where there were many opportunities to catch fish. There were times when we caught many fish and there were times when we came up empty. Whether we were successful in our quest of reeling in fish or not, I was still happy because I was spending time with my father. It was also great to experience the warmth of the sun on my face, gaze upon the blue water and peer into the distant horizon. When most people talk about fishing, they confuse the word fishing with catching.

Fishing will eventually lead to catching but the two words are not the same. Those who never learn to fully grasp the process of going fishing and only focus on the catching part will get easily frustrated. They will be the ones who are only result oriented and never learn to appreciate the fellowship and the enjoyment of the fishing experience.

As we seek the Lord, we begin to enjoy the process of seeking Him. We get excited about spending time with Him. When I am able to quiet my soul in the presence of God, He begins to speak to me. I ask the Lord what is on His heart. Like fishing, we can cheapen our experience in His presence if we only see spending time with God as some sort of conquest for answers. People who only approach God for what they can get from Him will never be able to have the intimacy that He desires with them.

When two people are truly in love, talking becomes natural to them. Gift giving and sacrificing for each other is also normative for people in love. I could list many things but there is something else that people do when they are in love that gets overlooked at times. They gaze upon or behold one another. I remember hearing a story about the late great evangelist, Dr. Billy Graham. Billy and his wife Ruth shared such affection for each other that when she was bedridden shortly before her transition, they would spend long periods of time just staring at each other. They did not need to say a word. They just sat there and enjoyed each other's presence. King David gave us a beautiful picture of the way he sought the Lord.

> *One thing I have desired of the Lord, that will I seek: That I may dwell in the house of the Lord All the days of my life, to behold the beauty of the Lord...* (Psalm 27:4 NKJV)

This passage in Scripture has become my life verse. Like Billy and Ruth Graham, we need not fill our prayer closets with words at all times. We need to spend time just beholding the *beauty of the Lord*. As we spend time beholding the Lord, we are changed in His presence. The glory of God begins to rest on us and we reflect His glory. The Apostle Paul wrote about this in his second letter to the church at Corinth.

> *But we all, with unveiled face, beholding as in a mirror the glory*
> *of the Lord, are being transformed into the same image from*
> *glory to glory, just as by the Spirit of the Lord.*
> (2 Corinthians 3:18 NKJV)

In the immediate context of this verse, Paul alluded to Moses and the children of Israel. Moses had to place a veil over his face because it was so bright due to him beholding the presence of God. Paul describes this glory as fading glory (2 Corinthians 3:12). We are blessed to be under the new covenant where we can constantly go from one degree of glory to another so that we are changed more into the image of Christ. It is the will of the Father that we spend time beholding the Lord Jesus because God has predestined us to be conformed to His likeness (Romans 8:29).

To use another example from the marriage relationship, there have been many times when there have been people wed for so many years that they begin to even look like each other. There has been scientific research undertaken to address this phenomenon. University of Michigan psychologist Robert Zajonc conducted a test to see whether or not two married people in love began to resemble one another after being together for a number of years.[15] Amber Angelle dissected the reason why older couples began to look alike in her assessment of Robert Zajonc.

"Zajonc suggested that older couples looked more alike because people in close contact mimic each other's facial expressions. In other words, if your partner has a good sense of humor and laughs a lot, he or she will probably develop laugh lines around their mouth—and so will you."[16]

Before I went into ministry many years ago, my pastor had a saying that has stayed with me until this present day. He would always remind the congregation that they would become like what they worshipped. In one sense, his admonishment encouraged us to keep going hard after God to become more like Jesus. There was also a strong warning, however, not to spend all of our time partaking of things that would make us desire other things more than God. As we spend time beholding the face of God, we will begin to mimic Jesus as we become more and more like who we are worshipping. As we are being transformed in God's presence, the people that we come in contact with start to desire more of God because they are attracted to the God inside of us.

The Importance of Prayer in Past Revivals

Azusa Street Revival

Though I believe in the sovereignty of God and know with all my heart that the Lord can send a fresh wave of revival glory anytime He wills, God often chooses to move in response to our prayers.

---

15 Amber Angelle, "Why Do Couples Start to Look Like Each Other," // www.livescience.com, (June 26, 2010).

16 Ibid.

If My people who are called by My name will humble themselves, and pray and seek My face, and turn from their wicked ways, then I will hear from heaven, and will forgive their sin and heal their land. (2 Chronicles 7:14 NKJV)

As a lover of Church history, I have been studying past moves of the Holy Spirit for many years. Though some can probably make a case that revival is ultimately based on a sovereign act of God, the common ingredient that I have observed in every case is that participants were hungry for God and sought the Lord in prayer. One such movement that has always fascinated me has been the Azusa Street Revival. As I mentioned previously, the leader of the revival, William J. Seymour, was a humble man fully yielded to the Holy Spirit.

Sometimes we can romanticize past moves of God by only focusing on the results of the revival. Azusa Street had great outcomes. Many people who attended were baptized in the Holy Spirit, Pentecostal denominations were formed, and millions of Pentecostals and Charismatic Christians today trace their roots directly or indirectly to the revival. I do not want to diminish the impact or fruit of past moves of God. How would we ever be able to discern a move of the Spirit if we did not closely examine what a movement produced? What I am arguing in this book is that if the Church of Jesus Christ spent more time focusing on the journey and preparation for revival, we would be more prepared for the glory that the Holy Spirit wants to release in the Church.

William J. Seymour, leader of the Azusa Street revival, was a man whose heart was prepared by God to lead a move of the Holy Spirit. Before Seymour was ever associated with Azusa Street and the revival that ensued in Los Angeles from 1906-1909, where he "conducted three services a day, seven days a week, where thousands of seekers received the baptism of the Holy Spirit,"[17] God prepared the soil of his heart. John G. Lake, a contemporary of Seymour and "Apostle to Africa," commented in detail about William J. Seymour in a sermon he preached on spiritual hunger. Lake even quoted Seymour and gave insight into the Azusa leader's prayer life before the revival broke out in Los Angeles.

> Later Brother {Charles Fox} Parham was preaching in Texas. A coloured man came into his meeting by the name of Seymour. In a hotel in Chicago he related his experience to Brother Tom and myself. I want you to see the hunger in that coloured man's soul. He said he was a waiter in a restaurant and preaching to a church of coloured people. He knew God as Saviour, as the sanctifier. He knew the power of God to heal. But as he listened to Parham he became convinced of a bigger thing, the baptism of the Holy Ghost. He went on to Los Angeles without receiving it, but he said he was determined to preach all of God he knew to the people. He said, "Brother, before I met Parham, such a hunger to have more of God was in my heart that I prayed for five hours a day for two and a half years. I got to Los Angeles, and when I got there the hunger was not less but more. I prayed, God, what can I do? And the Spirit said, pray more. But Lord, I am praying five hours a day now. I increased my hours of prayer to seven and prayed on for a year and a half more. I prayed God to give me what Parham preached, the real Holy Ghost and fire with tongues and love and power of God, like the apostles had."[18]

17 Fox, *William J. Seymour: Pioneer of the Azusa Street Revival*, 35.

18 John G. Lake, "Spiritual Hunger," *John G. Lake Writings* //www. healingrooms.com (December 11, 1924).

Lake helped his hearers grasp the importance of the role of prayer when mixed with spiritual hunger played in personal and corporate revival. I love this quote by Lake because it gives credence to the kind of sacrifice and commitment that provokes God to send a wave of His glory to hungry hearts. One of the main problems with early Pentecostal historians writing about Azusa Street was that they had a tendency to overlook Seymour's leadership and consecration to the Lord. It is my belief that Seymour's passion for intimacy with God in prayer primed his heart to lead and was instrumental in creating the atmosphere at Azusa Street for revival. Unfortunately, early Pentecostal historiography would argue that the event was only a sovereign move of God with no real leader.

Seymour was clearly the leader at Azusa Street and, as Lake stated, was already praying for five hours a day before increasing it to seven before he was baptized in the Holy Spirit. The baptism of the Holy Spirit changed everything for Seymour and was the main ingredient that drove thousands to frequent Azusa Street to bask in the presence of God as they spoke in other tongues.

A Word About the Baptism in the Holy Spirit

When William J. Seymour arrived in Los Angeles from Houston at the request of Neely Terry to help Julia Hutchins pastor a holiness church, an enthusiastic congregation greeted him and nightly meetings began at 9th and Santa Fe Streets.[19] The congregation's fervor for Seymour did not last long. Having been a student at Charles Fox Parham's training school during his tenure in Houston,[20] Seymour fully embraced Parham's teaching that glossalalia or speaking in tongues were the sign for those

---

19 Fox, *William J. Seymour: Pioneer of the Azusa Street Revival*, 34.
20 Ibid.,33.

who were truly baptized in the Holy Spirit. Seymour preached the Pentecostal doctrine with passion taking his text from Acts two verse four.[21] Unfortunately for Seymour, co-pastor Julia Hutchins rejected William's teaching on tongues as evidence of Spirit baptism and locked him out of the church with a padlock.[22]

With no job and no place to live, Seymour was invited to stay at the home of Richard and Ruth Asberry at 214 Bonnie Brae Street where he began nightly prayer meetings. The Holy Spirit fell on April 9, 1906 where several people were baptized with the Holy Spirit and spoke in tongues.[23] Ironically, though Seymour had been instrumental in helping others receive their personal Pentecost that day, Seymour was not baptized in the Holy Spirit with tongues until three days later.[24] It did not take long, however, for the news of Pentecost to spread at Bonnie Brae Street as Seymour used the front porch of the Asberry residence as a pulpit to preach to crowds on the street. The crowds swarmed so much to the point that the porch collapsed.[25] It was at this point that Seymour began the search for a bigger building, in anticipation of a mighty move of the Spirit. The search concluded when Seymour found an old building that was formerly an African Methodist Episcopal Church, but recently had been used as a stable and warehouse.[26] The address of the new location was 312 Azusa Street.

Though Seymour would later change in his stance on tongues as the primary sign of the baptism of the Holy Spirit to include

21 Ibid., 34.
22 Ibid., 34.
23 Charles Shumway, "A Critical History of Glossalalia" (PhD diss., Boston University, 1919), 116.
24 Ibid.,116; also see Douglas Nelson, "For Such a Time as This," 189.
25 Nelson, "For Such a Time as This," 191.
26 Fox, *William J. Seymour: Pioneer of the Azusa Street Revival*, 35.

more of an ethical component,[27] he maintained his stance that people must seek the baptism of the Holy Spirit.

> Beloved … we are not seeking for tongues, but we are seeking the baptism with the Holy Ghost and fire. And when we receive it, we shall be so filled with the Holy Ghost, that He Himself will speak in the power of the Spirit.[28]

Just as the Apostle Peter stood up boldly on the day of Pentecost to proclaim what the Spirit had done among them as three thousand souls were added to their number that day (Acts 2:14-38), Seymour was just as dauntless in promoting the Holy Spirit at Azusa. I believe the secret to Seymour's success at the Azusa Street Revival was his own experience with the baptism of the Holy Spirit and his continued resolve to keep his focus on the Lord without becoming overly preoccupied with tongues.

Seymour's understanding of the baptism of the Holy Spirit was broader than many of the participants and leaders who visited the Azusa meetings. For many, it was considered the tongues revival but not for Seymour. The Azusa leader summarized what he believed to be the essence of Pentecostal spirituality:

> The Pentecostal power, when you sum it all up, is just more of God's love. If it does not bring more love, it is simply

---

27 William J. Seymour, ed., "To the Baptized Saints," *The Apostolic Faith* 1, no. 9 (June to September 1907): 2. In this article that Seymour edited, he makes an argument for the importance of character or fruit of the Spirit for those claiming to be Spirit-filled because they could demonstrate tongues speaking. "Tongues are one of the signs that go with every baptized person, but it is not the real evidence of the baptism in the everyday life. Your life must measure with the fruits of the Spirit. If you get angry, or speak evil, or backbite, I care not how many tongues you may have, you have not the baptism of the Holy Spirit."

28 William J. Seymour, "The Baptism with the Holy Ghost," *The Apostolic Faith* 1, no. 6 (February to March 1907): 7.

a counterfeit. Pentecost means to live right in the 13th chapter of First Corinthians, which is the standard. When you live there, you have no trouble to keep salvation. This is Bible religion. It is not a manufactured religion. Pentecost makes us love Jesus more and love our brothers more. It brings us all into one common family.[29]

Seymour's stance on love as the essential mark of the baptism of the Holy Spirit not only stood in stark contrast to the classical Pentecostal view that evidential tongues be the primary proof of Spirit baptism, but the Azusa leader opened the door for Pentecostals and Charismatics to wrestle with what it really meant to be baptized in the Holy Spirit.

At this point I want to clarify that Seymour believed that every true believer who was baptized in the Holy Spirit would speak in other tongues because it was one of the signs of being filled with the Spirit.[30] Speaking in tongues allows us to speak directly to God and augments our prayer life. But for Seymour, this "New Pentecost" was the impetus for much more. For Seymour, the baptism of the Holy Spirit not only produced tongues but manufactured three more important things.

First, the baptism of the Holy Spirit caused Seymour and those who embraced his reconciling message of Pentecost to love Jesus more. When we as believers receive this baptism, we

---

29 William J. Seymour, ed., Untitled article, *The Apostolic Faith* 2, no. 13 (May 1908): 3.

30 William J. Seymour, ed., "To the Baptized Saints," *The Apostolic Faith* 1, no. 9 (June to September 1907): 2. In this article Seymour said the following: "Tongues are one of the signs that go with every baptized person, but it is not the real evidence of the baptism in the every day life. Your life must measure with the fruits of the Spirit. If you get angry, or speak evil, or backbite, I care not how many tongues you may have, you have not the baptism of the Holy Spirit."

desire to spend more time in prayer getting to know our Lord and Savior better. Our hunger for God begins to grow and we become more like who we are worshipping. In other words, the truth that God is love holds even greater significance for those who have experienced the baptism in the Holy Spirit because they begin to embody the love of the Father toward God and others (1 John 4:8).

Secondly, those who are baptized with the Spirit increase in love for one another. Seymour and the Azusa faithful not only grew in their love for God but for each other. That is why Seymour believed that true spirit-filled believers could reflect a lifestyle strait out of chapter thirteen of 1 Corinthians 13 which states:

Though I speak with the tongues of men and of angels, but have not love, I have become sounding brass or a clanging cymbal. And though I have the gift of prophecy, and understand all mysteries and all knowledge, and though I have all faith, so that I could remove mountains, but have not love, I am nothing. And though I bestow all my goods to feed the poor, and though I give my body to be burned, but have not love, it profits me nothing. Love suffers long and is kind; love does not envy; love does not parade itself, is not puffed up; does not behave rudely, does not seek its own, is not provoked, thinks no evil; does not rejoice in iniquity, but rejoices in the truth; bears all things, believes all things, hopes all things, endures all things. Love never fails. But whether there are prophecies, they will fail; whether there are tongues, they will cease; whether there is knowledge, it will vanish away. For we know in part and we prophesy in part. But when that which is perfect has come, then that which is in part will be done away. When I was a child, I spoke as a child, I understood as a child, I thought as a child; but when I became a man, I put away childish things. For now, we see in a mirror, dimly, but then face to face. Now I know in part, but then I shall know just as I also am known. And now abide faith, hope, love, these three; but the greatest of these is love. (1 Corinthians 13:1–13 NKJV)

Thirdly, according to Seymour, the baptism in the Holy Spirit produced the fruit of unity. One of the greatest miracles at the Azusa Street revival was the interracial harmony between the races. Azusa participant and chronicler Frank Bartleman coined the phrase: "The 'color line' was washed away in the blood."[31] The revival at the Azusa Street mission stood in contrast to the culture of racism and Jim Crow laws that was the norm during the early 1900's. Blacks and whites prayed and worshipped together under the leadership of a black pastor. Though the interracial togetherness that the Azusa participants enjoyed would later succumb to theological controversy and wilt under the increasing pressure of race politics in America, the Azusa Street Revival still stands as a wonderful example of what the baptism of the Holy Spirit can produce in the lives of the people of God.

Brownsville Revival

Historically God has answered the desperate cries of His people. This is what caused me to be filled with expectation as our church family at Brownsville Assembly of God cried out for revival. In fact, the Lord told me that as we made His house a house of prayer, He would pour out His Spirit in a powerful way. This is exactly what happened.[32] —John Kilpatrick

31 Frank Bartleman, *Azusa Street* (South Plainfield, NJ: Bridge Publishing, 1980), 54.

32 Michael Brown, John Kilpatrick and Larry Sparks, *The Fire that Never Sleeps: Keys to Sustaining Personal Revival* (Shippensburg, PA: Destiny Image Publishers, 2015), Kindle, 30.

Like Azusa Street, the Brownsville Revival in Pensacola, Florida under the leadership of Pastor John Kilpatrick and late Evangelist Steve Hill, was another bonafide move of God that had prayer as its foundation. In the quote above, John Kilpatrick, former pastor of Brownsville Assembly of God, was given an instruction by the Lord. That instruction was to make 'His (God's) house a house of prayer' and God would pour out His Spirit in a powerful way.

The Lord was faithful to the obedience of John Kilpatrick and Brownsville Assembly of God. On Father's Day, June 18th 1995, the Brownsville Revival was born, as Evangelist Steve Hill was invited to preach that day. For the next five years from 1995 to 2000, Pensacola, Florida became the epicenter for spiritual renewal as thousands of people flooded the southern city. Lost people were saved, backsliders came back to God, believers were refreshed in the presence of God, missionaries were sent out, and people were healed emotionally and physically. An estimated 4.5 million people converged upon Pensacola to take part in revival services at Brownsville Assembly of God.[33]

Similar to Azusa Street, Brownsville had lasting fruit of revival. Not only did the revival birth a missionary movement but it conceived the Brownsville Revival Ministry School—now named Fire School of Ministry. Though I have mentioned the importance of prayer that prepared Brownsville to receive an outpouring of the Holy Spirit, let's dig a bit deeper into the kind of praying that brought about the revival.

---

33 Ibid, 35.

Focused Prayer

Many pastors and believers have prayed for revival for several years but have not been able to experience a touch of God in their own lives, let alone the church they attend. As one studies the Brownsville Revival, it appears that one of the important elements was praying specifically for revival to happen. John Kilpatrick stated the following leading up to the revival:

> "When we started praying for revival at Brownsville, I knew the Lord was going to do something. I was confident He was going to pour out His Spirit. He is faithful to respond to the hungry and He is trustworthy to answer the cries of His people. The Bible tells us this, time after time."[34]

Pastor Kilpatrick and the Brownsville faithful were singularly focused on praying for a move of God. Prayer for revival was not just one more topic in prayer right after a prayer for world peace. Kilpatrick pressed into the Lord for a mighty move of the Spirit. Brownsville Assembly of God focused their attention on one thing—revival. Larry Sparks made an excellent observation about the priority of making revival a lifestyle.

> "For some, praying for revival has become one prayer request among many others. We pray for revival in the church and then we go on to pray for our friends who have lost their jobs. Revival is not something we can take or leave. A day is coming when four songs, a sermon, and an offering simply will not work anymore. Perhaps this model has been functional for a season, but in an hour of deep darkness, we

---

34 John Kilpatrick et.al, *The Fire that Never Sleeps*, Kindle, 29.

need to be a people who carry the light of the Kingdom. This will only happen as Christians live revival lifestyles."[35]

In essence, we as believers should continue to cry out for revival in our nation but we should also understand that we need to "be a revival." Sparks added, that "prayer for revival starts with being so gripped by Heaven's vision of the Christian life that everything you have embraced as normal becomes unacceptable." [36]As we rid ourselves of distractions and set our hearts to just know the Lord, we gain heaven's perspective in everything. We become so consumed with God that we begin to pray the agenda of heaven. This is what happened to John Kilpatrick and one major reason I believe God chose him to pastor a historic move of the Holy Spirit.

Long before Brownsville, God began preparing the soil of John Kilpatrick's heart to fulfill his destiny. Having been called by God to preach at the tender age of fourteen, Kilpatrick learned the importance of having a strong prayer life from his spiritual father and mentor, Pastor Raymond C. (R.C.) Wetzel. Unfortunately, John's natural father was abusive and abandoned him and his mother when he was only twelve. John Kilpatrick told the story of how the Lord brought Pastor Wetzel into his life.

> After I was called to preach at age fourteen, Brother Wetzel came to my mother and asked, "Would you let me take your son and teach him how to pray?" I remember standing there and thinking to myself, "Man, I'm not called to pray—I'm called to preach!" But it would appear he knew something

---

35 Ibid.,44.
36 Ibid., 44.

I didn't. Revival is not birthed through preaching, but through prayer.[37]

The time that John Kilpatrick spent with Pastor Wetzel was invaluable because he learned an important lesson that many preachers today have yet to learn—the primacy of prayer. Kilpatrick was forever transformed by Brother Wetzel's commitment to disciple and train an aspiring young preacher to always seek the Lord in prayer. What would happen today if older preachers and leaders would take more time to invest in the lives of our young people? Perhaps the senior pastor could volunteer to teach children's church one Sunday a month. Church leadership should also consider doubling the overall annual youth budget or simply inviting the youth to meet with the pastor for prayer and fellowship.

As young John Kilpatrick continued to pray with Pastor Wetzel, something happened that would change his life forever. What happened was an angelic visitation that manifested the glory of God. Kilpatrick described the encounter in detail below.

It was around midnight. We were walking around the sanctuary, praying for our church, our families, and our friends. This was definitely one of those nights we needed to "pray through." Police officers showed up routinely at the church building to make sure each door was securely locked. That night two angels broke into the church through those locked doors. This is a literal account of what I saw. This was not a vision of the mind or even an open vision. I saw the angels with my natural eyes. Both of the sanctuary doors

37 Ibid., 109.

were flung open—doors that had been bolted and locked. I can still hear the loud pop of the tin doorknob hitting the plaster walls. All seventeen of us looked up to see two powerful-looking angels walk through the entrance. One turned like a solider and went to the right side in the back of the sanctuary. He stood there solemnly, filling that area from the floor to the ceiling. Right after him, the other marched by, turned like a soldier, and went to the left side of the church. He, too, stood solemnly, his presence reaching from floor to ceiling...To this very day—and at the time of writing this book, I am sixty-four—fifty years later, I can picture it as though it was just yesterday. That one encounter is forever etched into my mind...Reflecting on my encounter, I remember that when the angels left, the building was absolutely saturated with the power of God. Brother Wetzel slowly stood and walked toward the back of the church to close the doors. Like little children fearing for their safety, each of us followed on his heels as he made his way to the doors. When we got back to the area where the angels had been positioned, we all fell like dominos under the power of the Spirit. The residue of power in that area was so strong, we could not stand under its weight... That was my first supernatural experience. It made such a profound impression on me that it became a benchmark for the rest of my life—and the rest of my ministry. Because I saw and experienced the genuine, nothing else would ever satisfy me.[38]

This visitation forever ruined John Kilpatrick and he could never settle for church as usual. The presence of God became his

---

38 Ibid., 115-118.

new normal. It is amazing how much we seem to get done in churches today without the presence of God in our midst. We all need to be ruined in the presence of God so that our paradigm can change.

Kilpatrick's encounter with the heavenly visitors was the thing that the Lord reminded him of shortly before revival broke out at Brownsville. The Holy Spirit gave the Pensacola leader the following directive: "If you will return to the God of your childhood—if you will make this a house of prayer—I will pour out my Spirit here."[39] John Kilpatrick demonstrated his obedience to this directive of the Lord by adjusting the Sunday night service format. He decided to make room to accommodate the Holy Spirit by changing the usual Sunday night service and began making himself available to pray for anyone wanting to be baptized in the Holy Spirit. Kilpatrick recorded that on that first Sunday night over one hundred people came to receive the baptism.[40]

The Lord made it clear to John Kilpatrick that prayer would now be the priority for Brownsville and that he could not go back to being "normal." The Brownsville Revival leader made the following statement about the impact of prayer on the revival:

> The Holy Spirit wants to move in every single church community in the world. This is a fact. The reason He does not is because many of these communities are unwilling to host Him and cater to His preferences. My decision to integrate Sunday night prayer meetings into the culture at Brownsville was monumental in preparing us for revival.[41]

39 Ibid., 124.
40 Ibid., 124.
41 Ibid., 124.

If the Body of Christ is to prepare for the glory that God desires to release in our churches, particularly in the United States of America, we must begin to accommodate the Holy Spirit by making our places of worship into houses of prayer again. We cannot continue to think that four songs, announcements and a sermon will make us ready for revival. Prayer must become a priority. We must display tenacity by our willingness to persevere in prayer in spite of how many people attend the prayer service. We must make the church a house of prayer!

4

A Persistent Heart

I believe that perseverance is essential and the trademark of those who receive a mighty outpouring of the Holy Spirit. In our society, we have great regard for individuals who have persevered to overcome seemingly impossible circumstances. We see this trait in Olympic athletes who train for years to become the best of the best in their respective areas of expertise. When I played football in high school and as I have watched the sport on television, I remember the announcers and coaches mentioning that certain players had "motors."

What did having a motor mean? Being told that you had a motor was actually one of the highest compliments you could give to a football player. To be given this label in sports meant that the individual demonstrated such tenacity in how they approached the game that they would outwork their opponents in a game, on the practice field and were always motivated to give their best. These kinds of athletes were the most respected people on the team.

I have adopted this "motor" mindset in the way that I approach my life and ministry. Persistence is what we need in order to get to new realms of the Spirit. There is always opposition in our way to any spiritual breakthrough. We must develop perseverance if we are to see revival come to our personal lives, ministries and churches. I love the story about Jacob in the book of Genesis.

> *Then Jacob was left alone; and a Man wrestled with him until the breaking of day. Now when He saw that He did not prevail against him, He touched the socket of his hip; and the socket of Jacob's hip was out of joint as He wrestled with him. And He said, "Let Me go, for the day breaks." But he said, "I will not let You go unless You bless me!"* (Genesis 32:24–26 NKJV)

As we examine one of the Bible's most mysterious narratives, it becomes clear from the context that Jacob is not just wrestling with an average man. He was wrestling with God and refused to let go until he received the blessing. Jacob left this encounter as a changed man. His name was changed from Jacob which means supplanter or deceiver to Israel, which means he who strives with God and prevails. The encounter that Jacob had with the Lord also cost him something—he would now walk with a limp for the rest of his life. As we draw closer to the Lord, He develops in us a perseverance that enables us to pay the price for revival. Nothing matters to us except knowing Him and experiencing all that He has for us. The Lord Jesus stressed an important lesson about persistence in Matthew's gospel:

> *"Ask, and it will be given to you; seek, and you will find; knock, and it will be opened to you. For everyone who asks receives, and he who seeks finds, and to him who knocks it will be opened."* (Matthew 7:7–8 NKJV)

In verse seven of Matthew, there are three important Greek imperatives: ask, seek and knock. These words are also in the present tense and can be interpreted in this context as *"keep asking, keep seeking, and keep knocking."* Petitioning our Heavenly Father is meant to be perpetual. I believe that many believers are hungry for God and are willing to persevere in prayer. Right now many people are being given special grace by the Lord to persevere in what many older saints used to label as "praying through." In spite of their circumstances and the opposition facing them, these people are continuing to ask, seek and knock on heaven's door until they receive a victory breakthrough in the realm of the Spirit.

As I mentioned earlier, these persistent people have been tested and have walked through the crucible of character. The word quit means absolutely nothing to them. It's interesting how important language is to each generation. As one person who is part of Generation X growing up in the 70's and 80's, I would hear phrases such as "tarrying for the Holy Ghost" or "unction from the Holy Spirit." The first phrase, tarrying for the Holy Ghost was the term I was most familiar with when we (my family) attended a small African-American Pentecostal church in Brooklyn, New York in early 80's.

It was at this church that I first learned the importance of persevering in the things of God. The name of the church was Faithway Church of Deliverance, led by Pastor "Mother" Mary Bryant. As a teenager, I remember arriving from Queens in our station wagon to Brother Junior Bryant's Sunday School class. As soon as the teaching time was over, there would be a time of tarrying at the altar. Folding chairs were set up on the right side of the little storefront church so that people could seek the Lord in prayer before the official call to worship.

One particular Sunday, as we began our usual tarrying time, I came to the altar and kneeled in prayer. I began to experience the joy of the Lord at first and felt the love of God like I never felt before in my young life. It was wonderful. Then suddenly, something unusual happened. I had been enjoying the presence of God for probably around twenty minutes and was the only person still at the makeshift folding chair altar. During praise and worship, that location was also used as the choir "loft." Mother Bryant began telling me to "say yes to the Lord." I can remember this loving woman, now in heaven, being so patient with me. It did not matter to her who was arriving at that time for the morning service. She stayed right there with me at that altar encouraging me to yield to the Holy Spirit. As she continued to work with me, it became increasingly evident that there was something wrong. Every time I tried to say "yes" to the Lord, I could only say "yeah" in a joking, kind of mocking way.

At this point, the battle was on. This loving sweet woman did something that I had never seen before in my short life. With the intensity and love of a mother protecting her only child from a predator, she said, "come out of him!" When she said these words, another voice came out of me that screamed as if it were in pain. I was afraid and tried to speak but every time I made an attempt to say something, the voice inside of me roared in agony.

Pastor Bryant, along with my father and the other ministry leaders, were tenacious. Mother Bryant got on the floor with me and fought for my deliverance. Needless to say, we did not have a traditional service that day. Pastor Bryant worked with me the entire service until the evil spirit came out of me. After the ordeal was over, she hugged me and the congregation rejoiced over my deliverance.

As I reflect upon Mother Bryant and the Faithway Church of Deliverance congregation, I am forever grateful that I was placed in the care of a godly woman who persevered for my deliverance that day over thirty years ago. Although my time with Mother Bryant was impactful to my spiritual formation, this story underscores the importance of persistence. We must be careful not to adopt a "microwave culture" that makes us so impatient that if we do not have immediate results in something, we simply give up.

I believe wholeheartedly that the glory of God is about to be poured out in a fresh way on planet earth but I believe that the ones who will experience this outpouring will be the people who have prepared their hearts. They are the ones who have developed persistence in the face of overwhelming trials and opposition. People like Pastor Bryant had no issue spending an entire Sunday morning service with me because she spent countless hours with God and developed endurance. Our Lord talked about the importance of persistence.

> Then He spoke a parable to them, that men always ought to pray and not lose heart, saying: "There was in a certain city a judge who did not fear God nor regard man. Now there was a widow in that city; and she came to him, saying, 'Get justice for me from my adversary.' And he would not for a while; but afterward he said within himself, 'Though I do not fear God nor regard man, yet because this widow troubles me I will avenge her, lest by her continual coming she weary me.'" Then the Lord said, "Hear what

the unjust judge said. And shall God not avenge His own elect who cry out day and night to Him, though He bears long with them? I tell you that He will avenge them speedily. Nevertheless, when the Son of Man comes, will He really find faith on the earth?"

(Luke 18:1–8 NKJV)

This is one of my favorite parables because it is so encouraging. Luke makes it clear from the onset that the purpose of this story is to motivate people to never give up in spite of their circumstances. In the parable, the Lord Jesus focuses on two main characters—the unjust judge and the widow. As the story unfolds we see that the widow eventually receives justice from the judge regarding her adversary due to her persistence and not based upon the character of the magistrate. The judge grants her request for selfish reasons. He is not interested in her welfare but only caves in to her petition because he does not want to be inconvenienced by her continually asking for justice. I am so thankful that my God is the righteous judge who does not just accommodate my persistence in prayer because of impatience or because He is tired of me. The Lord gives me justice because He is just. As I cry out to him, He answers me because He loves me.

The Lord Jesus teaches us an important lesson here. Those who stay in faith by being persistent in prayer to the Father will receive justice and breakthrough if they will not quit. The same is true for those who refuse to give up trusting God for revival. If we continue to fix our hearts on the Lord, we will experience the glory of God. I am reminded of what the writer of Hebrews states about endurance to his readers:

So do not throw away this confident trust in the Lord. Remember the great reward it brings you! Patient endurance is what

you need now, so that you will continue to do God's will. Then
you will receive all that he has promised. "For in just a little while,
the Coming One will come and not delay. And my righteous
ones will live by faith. But I will take no pleasure in anyone who
turns away."

But we are not like those who turn away from God to their own
destruction. We are the faithful ones, whose souls will be saved.
(Hebrews 10:35–39 NLT)

Though the writer of Hebrews is encouraging believers in
the context of this passage to walk in patient endurance as they
wait in expectancy for the coming of the Lord, we can also apply
this passage to other areas of our Christian walk, particularly as it
relates to revival. Those who have remained faithful by believing
that a mighty move of God is imminent are a remnant. I believe
they are in the minority but God will use them to spread revival
fire to millions around the world.

While speaking to a Christian publisher friend of mine,
he informed me recently that books about the topic of revival
were not selling as well. So why would I write another book on
revival? The fact that book sales on the subject of revival are
in decline should cause us to speak on it more and not less. In
essence, this is precisely why we need to continue to write and
talk about revival. Just as the writer of Hebrews admonished his
fellow believers to not "throw away" their confidence, I want to
encourage my fellow believers to keep pursuing the Lord. We
must not give into the apathy and the difficulties of our times.
In verse 36 in the passage above, the word endurance in Greek is
the word hupŏmŏnē. This word used in this context also implies
steadfast endurance in the midst of difficult circumstances.

When we look at the landscape of our country with all of its political and socioeconomic division, we can take on an apathetic attitude about revival ever coming to our nation. We must realize though that God often sends a mighty outpouring in the midst of seemingly impossible circumstances. I am reminded of the context in which the great reformer Martin Luther nailed his Ninety Theses to the Wittenberg door, spearheading the Protestant Reformation. At the time of Luther's writing of the theses, there was gross immorality in the Church. Abusive clergy were selling plenary indulgences, which were essentially certificates of forgiveness believed to reduce time in purgatory for sins committed by the purchasers or their loved ones.

Though Luther would later be excommunicated in 1521 and would champion the doctrine of justification by faith, October 31st 1517 is considered to be the start of the Reformation and is commemorated annually as Reformation Day. Luther and many others had no clue how much the entire landscape of the Church would change so radically due to the posting of the theses, but God chose this as the time for transformation. What God did in the Reformation should encourage us to persevere and not yield to a spirit of discouragement regarding these turbulent times. God is still on the throne.

We must realize that persistence is essential, especially in the last days because Scripture predicted that one day there would be scoffers who would say, *"Where is the promise of His coming? For since the fathers fell asleep, all things continue as they were from the beginning of creation."* (2 Peter 3:4 NKJV)

Though the Apostle Peter in this epistle is reminding his readers that God is being patient with humankind and delaying judgement, he also admonished his audience that the day of the Lord would come when they least expected it, like a thief in the night. Peter, however, also encouraged believers to look forward to the day of Christ's return with great anticipation, even hastening the suddenly of God (2 Peter 3:12). We should have this same anticipation about the move of the Holy Spirit and not be discouraged by the scoffers who are critical of those of us who continue to prophesy boldly about the greater glory being poured out on the earth. We must allow the Holy Spirit to develop persistence in us and be thankful for what the Lord is already doing in our midst.

whole. One of the things that we must be aware of when this face of Jezebel is at work is that you literally feel like something is squeezing the life out of you. It will make you want to quit before a Holy Spirit outpouring. The squeezing from this face of Jezebel may come in the form of nagging sicknesses, lack of financial resources, exiting church members or a combination of these happening all at the same time.

A few years ago, the Holy Spirit gave me a dream to give me insight into the way that Jezebel works within the Body of Christ. One night I was dreaming that I was lying down in what appeared to be a watery grave. I was amazed at how much peace that I felt while I was lying in this watery grave. If I was in the natural, it would have been absolutely terrifying. As I was lying there, I began to say in my mind, "I know that I am going to be raised." This went on for several minutes. Then suddenly, I began to get up. As I looked down at my feet, I saw dead fish all over the place. I then looked into an incredibly foul pool and saw what appeared to be leeches on parts of my face. I pulled them off and then noticed something to my right that was even more startling. To my right was a huge python snake that appeared to be sleeping. I knew instantly that the snake was responsible for all the dead fish in the pool and was poisoning everything. I began to look for something to kill the snake before it woke up. As the snake was starting to wake up, the dream ended. When I awoke from the dream, I began to pray and the Holy Spirit began to give me the interpretation. The dead fish represented people in the Body of Christ that had succumbed to this spirit. Their spiritual lives had become limited just like the dead fish in the watery grave. The enemy had squeezed the life right out of them by suffocating

—— 5 ——

A Thankful Heart

Since we are receiving a Kingdom that is unshakable, let us be thankful and please God by worshiping him with holy fear and awe. (Hebrews 12:28 NLT)

As I think about the Thanksgiving holiday that we have just observed at the writing of this book at the Fox residence with my loving wife, two teenage children and my extended family, I am thankful for the wonderful time of fellowship and the many blessings the Lord has bestowed on us this past year. I am aware, however, that giving thanks during Thanksgiving time can be easy for people when things are going well for them. It is great that many families across the United States take time to pause around the dinner table to reflect on their many blessings. The problem for many people is that thankfulness has become something that is connected to an event or their current situation instead of a lifestyle for the other three hundred and sixty-four days of the year. It is my belief that a heart prepared for revival is a thankful heart. It is a heart that continually appreciates and celebrates the presence of God no matter the circumstances.

Several years ago we (my wife and I) attended a Supernatural Fivefold Ministry School in Miami at King Jesus Ministry, under the leadership of Apostle Guillermo Maldonado. The Holy Spirit impacted my wife and me in a powerful way as we received a tremendous impartation to flow in signs, wonders and miracles. It was also during this time that I learned something extremely important about attracting and hosting the presence of God— thankfulness. Apostle Maldonado drove home the message that we needed to celebrate the presence of God in our midst and not just tolerate Him. I learned that the Holy Spirit manifests Himself wherever He is appreciated and when worshippers are grateful for His presence.

Gratefulness is an important aspect all throughout the Bible. I am reminded of the story of the ten lepers.

> *Now it happened as He went to Jerusalem that He passed through the midst of Samaria and Galilee. Then as He entered a certain village, there met Him ten men who were lepers, who stood afar off. And they lifted up their voices and said, "Jesus, Master, have mercy on us! "So when He saw them, He said to them, "Go, show yourselves to the priests." And so it was that as they went, they were cleansed. And one of them, when he saw that he was healed, returned, and with a loud voice glorified God, and fell down on his face at His feet, giving Him thanks. And he was a Samaritan. So Jesus answered and said, "Were there not ten cleansed? But where are the nine? Were there not any found who returned to give glory to God except this foreigner?" And He said to him, "Arise, go your way. Your faith has made you well."*
>
> (Luke 17:11–19 NKJV)

From the story of the ten lepers we gain tremendous insight into the mind of the Lord Jesus regarding the importance of thanksgiving. In this story, the only person to return to Jesus after he was healed was a Samaritan. The implication was that the other nine men did not show gratitude for what Jesus had done for them. Bible scholars believe that the other nine lepers were Jews who probably represented the attitude of ungratefulness and sense of entitlement of the nation of Israel. In his great mercy, the Lord Jesus still cleansed the lepers in spite of their ingratitude. The Samaritan, who was despised by Jews, received much more from the Lord. Due to the fact that the Samaritan returned to give thanks for his healing, Scripture states that his faith made him "well." The word for well is the word sozo in the Greek. It actually means whole or saved. In essence, the nine ingrates only received physical healing but the foreigner/Samaritan received physical healing and salvation. He was able to enjoy fellowship and relationship due to an attitude of gratitude.

I love the story about the lepers because it displays the importance of a thankful heart. The man in the story was made whole and began a relationship with the Lord based on his display of gratefulness. I believe that thankfulness is a major component in preparing for and sustaining a move of the Holy Spirit. As I alluded to earlier, the manifest presence of God shows up whenever He is celebrated. As we celebrate the Lord and build an atmosphere of thankfulness, our worship environment becomes a holy habitation. We become hosts of the manifest presence of God.

Throughout history God has sent mighty outpourings of the Spirit that we have defined as revivals. I have spent a good portion of my life studying them and have alluded to several in this book. Some of these revivals lasted for several years and others have been much shorter. These revivals could be described as "visitations" of the manifest presence of God. These moves were labeled visitations because they were similar to a guest who showed up at our home to stay with us for two weeks. The guest had a start date and end date when they left. How does the Church of the Lord Jesus shift from a temporary revival into a sustainable culture of revival? Thankfulness!

We must create an atmosphere of thanksgiving for what the Lord has done and is doing in our midst. It sounds too simple or too good to be true, doesn't it? The Psalms give us several clues about the significance of thankfulness as it pertains to attracting the presence of God. Enclosed is an oft used passage on the importance of thanksgiving in worship:

> Enter into His gates with thanksgiving, And into His courts with praise. Be thankful to Him and bless His name. For the Lord is good; His mercy is everlasting, And His truth endures to all generations. (Psalm 100:4–5 NKJV)

What we gather from this passage is the protocol for encountering God's presence—thanksgiving and praise. God wants to manifest himself in our worship services but many times He does not because the atmosphere is not conducive for His presence. People forget that God has already given us the spiritual etiquette for attracting the glory. As a pastor, I have experienced wonderful times of corporate worship when it seemed like everyone in attendance was on the same page so-to-speak regarding worship. The people came with a thankful heart and filled the atmosphere with praise. At those times, words of knowledge, healings, angelic visitations, miracles and preaching of the Word become easy. Why? The simple reason is that the glory of God filled the room because we had set the right atmosphere by being united in worship.

Unfortunately, I have also experienced many times when it was difficult to preach or flow in the Holy Spirit because there was a tough spiritual atmosphere due to worry, unthankfulness, religiosity and selfishness. People came in with the wrong mindset. Their focus was not on the Lord but myopically centered on themselves and their problems. If believers would simply set their affections on the Lord instead of depending on the leader or another person to give them a word about their life, they would create the correct atmosphere for the glory of God. Every need that they have would be met in the presence of God.

I believe that the glory of God is about to be poured out on the earth like never before and that worship will play an essential role as to who will experience the manifest presence of God. There are several prophets who believe that this last move will be the Glory of the Father. I believe this as well. I also agree with what Bill Johnson said about the importance of the presence of God. "We gather around a sermon; Israel, however, camped around the Presence of God."[42]

Bill Johnson is not advocating the removal of preaching from worship but I believe he is arguing for the centrality of the presence of God above everything else. We will always need the Word of God. This next move of God, however, will be about the glory of the Father. As stated previously, thanksgiving is the entry point into the presence of God. It is not just the starting

---

42 Larry Sparks and Ana Werner, *Accessing the Greater Glory: A Prophetic Invitation to New Realms of Holy Spirit Encounter* (Destiny Image: 2019), Kindle, Loc. 2568.

point, however, but it is also the sticking point and how we access deeper realms of the Spirit.

Let me explain. As a husband and father of two teenage children, I am blessed when my children are thankful for the things that I do for them. When my children show gratitude and show their appreciation for me, it actually makes me want to do even more for them. I begin to give things to them that they had not even requested. Scripture states, however, that my best fathering is evil compared to God the Father (Matthew 7:11). God is a perfect Father who loves when His children spend time with Him. He wants to lavish us with His perfect love, especially when we demonstrate thankfulness and just want to be in His presence. True thankfulness gets the attention of heaven. The following parable is an example about the importance of thankfulness and gratitude from our Lord Jesus.

> Also He spoke this parable to some who trusted in themselves that they were righteous, and despised others: "Two men went up to the temple to pray, one a Pharisee and the other a tax collector. The Pharisee stood and prayed thus with himself, 'God, I thank You that I am not like other men—extortioners, unjust, adulterers, or even as this tax collector. I fast twice a week; I give tithes of all that I possess.' And the tax collector, standing afar off, would not so much as raise his eyes to heaven, but beat his breast, saying, 'God, be merciful to me a sinner!' I tell you, this man went down to his house justified rather than the other; for everyone who exalts himself will be humbled, and he who humbles himself will be exalted." (Luke 18:9–14 NKJV)

In the story above we observe two men going up to the temple to worship but only one man went truly in right standing with God. The Pharisee has an impressive résumé of service to the Lord. He is the kind of person that pastors love. He comes to prayer meeting and is generous in his giving. If he were attending a church today, he would be a trustee or on the elder board. He has one major problem though. His heart is not right towards God. He is prideful and self-righteous. Because he depends on his own righteousness, he cannot fully appreciate what God has done for him. The tax collector, however, has a different heart. He prays with humility and relies on the mercy of God instead of his own righteousness.

The tax collector is also able to practice true thankfulness because a person who relies solely on the goodness and mercy of God will be forever grateful to the Lord. The Lord Jesus goes into further detail about this concept in Luke's gospel account.

Then one of the Pharisees asked Him to eat with him. And He went to the Pharisee's house, and sat down to eat. And behold, a woman in the city who was a sinner, when she knew that Jesus sat at the table in the Pharisee's house, brought an alabaster flask of fragrant oil, and stood at His feet behind Him weeping; and she began to wash His feet with her tears, and wiped them with the hair of her head; and she kissed His feet and anointed them with the fragrant oil. Now when the Pharisee who had invited Him saw this, he spoke to himself, saying, "This Man, if He were a prophet, would know who and what manner of woman this is who is touching Him, for she is a sinner. "And Jesus answered and said to him, "Simon, I have something to say to you." So he said, "Teacher, say it." "There was a certain creditor who had two debtors. One owed five hundred denarii, and the other fifty. And when they had nothing with which to repay, he freely forgave them both. Tell Me, therefore, which of them will love him more?

"Simon answered and said, "I suppose the one whom he forgave more." And He said to him, "You have rightly judged. "Then He turned to the woman and said to Simon, "Do you see this woman? I entered your house; you gave Me no water for My feet, but she has washed My feet with her tears and wiped them with the hair of her head. You gave Me no kiss, but this woman has not ceased to kiss My feet since the time I came in. You did not anoint My head with oil, but this woman has anointed My feet with fragrant oil. Therefore I say to you, her sins, which are many, are forgiven, for she loved much. But to whom little is forgiven, the same loves little." (Luke 7:36–47 NKJV)

Once again we see contrasting positions. In the parable above, Jesus makes a correlation between two debtors and between Simon the Pharisee who invited Jesus to dinner and the sinful woman in the story. Simon most likely invited Jesus to dinner out of curiosity and to possibly find evidence for accusation. His lack of courtesy and appreciation for his "honored guest" was exposed by the sincere worship of the woman who was likely a prostitute. Her extravagant worship and humility was in stark contrast to the prideful attitude of the Pharisee. Knowing the heart of the Pharisee, Jesus then goes into the story of the two debtors, leaving no doubt in the mind of Simon and his other guests that he (Simon) represents the debtor forgiven of a small debt.

I believe that the two polar opposites in the story above represent a microcosm of the Church today. There are those in the Body of Christ who are like the woman and cannot express their love and appreciation enough for what the Lord has done for them. They are former drug users, prostitutes, sexually immoral, liars, etc. Their hearts have been prepared for the move of the Holy Spirit because they have thankful hearts. They have increased their spiritual capacity because they love spending time worshipping Jesus. They cannot get over what He has done for them.

At opposite sides of the spectrum, there are those in Body of Christ who represent Simon the Pharisee. They are avid church attenders, deacons, pastors, elders, and Christians from every walk of life. These people believe they are ready for a move of the Holy Spirit but their hearts need more preparation. They have left their first love and have become distracted. Like the Pharisee in the parable, they have not humbled themselves to truly worship the Lord. They are more concerned about keeping a position and status quo than truly expressing gratitude for their salvation. They are comparable to the "Loveless Church" of Ephesus in the book of Revelation.

> *"To the angel of the church of Ephesus write, 'These things says He who holds the seven stars in His right hand, who walks in the midst of the seven golden lampstands: "I know your works, your labor, your patience, and that you cannot bear those who are evil. And you have tested those who say they are apostles and are not, and have found them liars; and you have persevered and have patience, and have labored for My name's sake and have not become weary. Nevertheless, I have this against you, that you have left your first love. Remember therefore from where you have fallen; repent and do the first works, or else I will come to you quickly and remove your lampstand from its place—unless you repent."* (Revelation 2:1–5 NKJV)

Our Lord describes a church in Ephesus that has a passion for doctrinal purity and for exposing false teachers. The Lord

Jesus even commends their patience and hard work in ministry. What He has against them is they have traded passionate love for Jesus for lifeless orthodoxy. The church in Ephesus is warned of impending judgement if they do not repent and turn back to their "first love."

If we are to be ready for the great outpouring that God is about to send to the earth, we must repent for allowing our hearts to become calloused because of putting more emphasis on knowing the right things to say scripturally, hermeneutically and theologically rather than focusing on the person of Jesus. The sinful woman who washed the feet of Jesus represents where the Lord desires for His Church to be. The Lord desires a Church so filled with love and gratitude that their love is expressed openly in such extravagant ways that it changes atmospheres because of the fragrance of our worship to God. Like the woman in the story, the Church of the Lord Jesus Christ must not be ashamed to display love through radical acts of thanksgiving but must also have the courage to pay the price to experience the manifest presence of the God.

A Courageous Heart

"Now, Lord, look on their threats, and grant to Your servants that with all boldness they may speak Your word, by stretching out Your hand to heal, and that signs and wonders may be done through the name of Your holy Servant Jesus."

And when they had prayed, the place where they were assembled together was shaken; and they were all filled with the Holy Spirit, and they spoke the word of God with boldness."

(Acts 4:29–31 NKJV)

Having been warned, threatened and arrested for preaching in the name of Jesus by the Pharisees, Peter and John recite a beautiful prayer asking God for boldness in order to continue to fulfill the commission given to them by the Lord Jesus. The answer to their prayer for more courage was a resounding yes! The place was shaken and they spoke with boldness in spite of the spiritual warfare and spirit of intimidation that was at work in the religious leaders.

Like the early apostles, the Holy Spirit is preparing the hearts of believers in the Body of Christ to walk in boldness to stand against all forms of intimidation from the enemy. This final chapter will address courage. It takes a courageous heart to be able to stand up to the spiritual warfare that is waged against those who desire to participate in the glory that is about to be poured out all over the earth.

The apostle Paul, in Ephesians, gave us a clear understanding of the reality of spiritual warfare for every believer: *"For we do not wrestle against flesh and blood, but against principalities, against powers, against the rulers of the darkness of this age, against spiritual hosts of wickedness in the heavenly places"* (Ephesians 6:12 NKJV). While we must take heed of the actuality of this constant struggle, we need to understand the rules of engagement. In fact, the term "rules of engagement" is a military term that establishes the manner, conditions and circumstances in which the use of force, or actions which might be construed as provocative, may be applied.[43] In the same way that countries and nations establish rules of engagement in war, God has established the rules of engagement for war with the enemy. In his book entitled, *Needless Casualties of War*, John Paul Jackson admonished prayer warriors to understand the proper parameters of our delegated authority and argued that many Christians have become victims of war due to improper engagement in spiritual warfare.[44]

As believers God has given us authority or the right to exercise His power on the earth. Psalm 115:16 states: *"The heaven, even the heavens, are the LORD's; But the earth He has given to the children of*

---

43 NATO ROE MC 362/1.

44 John Paul Jackson, *Needless Casualties of War* (Flower Mound, TX: Streams Publications, 1999), 24.

men."This passage is important because it gives the parameters of man's dominion. Although the heavens and the earth belong to God, He has delegated the authority of the earth to humankind. You see this same theme in Genesis when God said: "...*Let Us make man in Our image, according to Our likeness; let them have dominion over the fish of the sea, over the birds of the air, and over the cattle, over all the earth and over every creeping thing that creeps on the earth.*" (Genesis 1:26 NKJV). Man lost this authority when Adam and Eve sinned and the right to rule God's creation on the earth was abdicated to Satan temporarily. The good news is that we have this authority back because of Jesus' sacrificial death on the cross for all mankind and His glorious resurrection. He took the keys from Satan and we now have that same authority through the name of Jesus that we had in the beginning in Genesis. The parameters are still the same. We have the right to cast out demons on the earth, calm storms, and utilize our authority over the creatures on the earth and in the sky. Where we get into trouble is when we do not allow the Holy Spirit to lead as it pertains to spiritual warfare in the second heaven. (I will explain more about being led by the Holy Spirit into spiritual warfare a bit later).

I was baptized in the Holy Spirit in my early twenties. It was awesome. I began to walk in a new dimension of power and authority. My prayer life grew tremendously and I would pray for hours at a time in my bedroom. It was during this time that I developed ideas about spiritual warfare that were not wise because of a spiritual mentor that I was following at the time. This person had a worldwide ministry and I had great respect for him. He had a powerful ministry in healing and deliverance. He walked in great authority in the Spirit. I would watch him war in the Spirit against demonic principalities and thought that it was normal for me to imitate him. I would pray strong prayers in warring tongues and sometimes I felt like I was invincible. I prayed like this for several years. I would command the demonic principalities in my region to obey. Little did I know that I was actually making myself and my family vulnerable to demonic counter attacks by doing this.

In his book, *Needless Casualties of War* John Paul Jackson shared a dream that he had that the Holy Spirit gave him about spiritual warfare that transformed my approach to spiritual combat. I have included the dream in detail below and it is entitled, "Throwing Hatchets at the Moon":

"It was night; the sky was blue-black except for a huge luminous moon that filled the horizon. In the remote blackness, several figures were silhouetted against the moon. Each figure stood on a circular platform and preached to a small group of people. With great emotion, leaders pointed and shouted at the moon, urging others to follow them. Gradually, each leader's platform rose higher as the crowds grew larger. Some platforms rose above the crowds to precarious heights. Others lifted only slightly off the ground. Resembling gunslingers, the leaders stood on the platforms with holsters strapped to their hips. But instead of guns in the holsters, there were hatchets tucked inside. As leaders began to preach, crowds of people gathered around them. Then, each leader grabbed a hatchet, waved it around, and hurled it at the moon. But the hatchet never hit the moon; it simply fell into the darkness that lay beyond. After some time, the leaders grew weary. Eventually, each lay down on his or her platform and fell asleep. Then with undetected stealth, several dark figures dropped off the moon's surface. They crawled up poles which held up platforms, sneaked over, and began to attack the leaders with extreme viciousness... "Somebody help me, I'm dying," someone pleaded. It was a terrifying sight and sound."[45]

Before Jackson woke up from the dream, he stated that the Lord spoke to him and gave the interpretation: "To attack principalities and powers over a geographic area can be as useless as throwing hatchets at the moon. And it can leave you open to unforeseen and unperceived attacks."[46] Due to my spiritual upbringing in spiritual warfare, I was attacking principalities over my city and it caused unforeseen attacks in my life. My wife came under attack in her body. My wife and I had just transitioned our family to the Washington DC area from Virginia Beach, Virginia to accept a pastorate in the Maryland suburbs. She was a healthy woman before coming to this church but now she suddenly came down with vertigo and had trouble with her nervous system. This lasted for four months. Her condition started right after my wife and I walked around the church praying and coming against the spiritual entity that was causing issues for us in the ministry and in the city. We had not just come to Maryland to pastor a church but we were believing for a mighty move of the Holy Spirit in the church and city that would affect the region.

The congregation began to get concerned because the wife of the pastor before me had died due to cancer. The thought that my wife's condition could worsen was in the back of my mind but I began to cast the thoughts down and bring them into subjection to Jesus. We understood that we had authority in the name of Jesus, but we kept getting attacked because we

45 Jackson, *Needless Casualties of War*, 31-33.
46 Ibid., 33.

were inexperienced in spiritual warfare. The church had other spiritual baggage with a long history with the spirit of Jezebel, (which I will address a bit later). We had taken authority over high ranking demonic principalities in our area over the heavens and they counterattacked us. I even began to see demonic apparitions in my bedroom at night while sleeping. We were attracting all of these unnecessary attacks due to not following the leading of the Holy Spirit nor respecting our opponents in the second heaven.

Three Heavens

The apostle Paul gave us some insight into the heavenly realms. He spoke in the third person about an experience that he had in the third heaven.

> *I know a man in Christ who fourteen years ago—whether in the body I do not know, or whether out of the body I do not know, God knows —such a one was caught up to the third heaven. And I know such a man —whether in the body or out of the body I do not know, God knows – how he was caught up into Paradise and heard inexpressible words, which it is not lawful for a man to utter.* (2 Corinthians 12:2-4 NKJV)

The fact that Paul was caught up in the third heaven implies that there is a first and second heaven. Most Bible scholars believe that the first heaven is earth's sky where birds fly. The second heaven is considered to be outer space where the sun, moon and stars give light to the earth (Genesis 15:5; Deuteronomy 4:19; Psalm 8:3 NKJV). The second heaven is also the place where Satan and high ranking demonic powers reside. As we previously mentioned, Ephesians 6:12 declares that we wrestle against "principalities, against powers, against the rulers of the darkness of this age, against spiritual hosts of wickedness in the heavenly places."

Satan himself in Scripture was given the title as the prince of the power of the air and is the spirit that is currently at work in those who are disobedient towards God (Ephesians 2:2).

The book of Daniel gives us a peek into the kinds of battles that occur in the second heaven and how important it is for us to pray so that the Lord can fight these battles for us. Daniel had prayed intensely for three weeks but had not had a breakthrough due to a demonic spirit that withheld an angel that was bringing back an answer to his prayers:

> *Suddenly, a hand touched me, which made me tremble on my knees and on the palms of my hands. And he said to me, "O Daniel, man greatly beloved, understand the words that I speak to you, and stand upright, for I have now been sent to you." While he was speaking this word to me, I stood trembling. Then he said to me, "Do not fear, Daniel, for from the first day that you set your heart to understand, and to humble yourself before your God, your words were heard; and I have come because of your words. "But the prince of the kingdom of Persia withstood me twenty-one days; and behold, Michael, one of the chief princes, came to help me, for I had been left alone there with the kings of Persia. Now I have come to make you understand what will happen to your people in the latter days, for the vision refers to many days yet to come."* (Daniel 10:10-14 NKJV)

As you can see from the passage above, there was a demonic prince that delayed the angel for twenty-one days. Daniel's prayer was heard by God from day one but there was a battle in the heavenly realm, which I believe to be the second heaven. What is interesting to note is that we never observe Daniel address any principalities to try to pull them down, but we do see Michael the archangel and chief prince coming to do warfare and get the other angel through to Daniel. This is an important point because I had taken on the task of doing this kind of warfare upon myself for many years. As believers we must understand that God is responsible for dispatching His angels to take charge over us and He will deal with the principalities and powers in the second heaven as we pray. We have been commissioned by him to deal with the enemy but we need to engage in spiritual warfare the right way.

Doing Spiritual Warfare the Right Way

How do we engage the enemy in a way that is appropriate? We are called to do warfare as Paul states in Ephesians 6:12. We are commanded to put on the whole armor of God (Ephesians 6:11). Paul specifies what this armor is all about in his letter to the Ephesians:

> *Therefore, take up the whole armor of God, that you may be able to withstand in the evil day, and having done all, to stand. Stand therefore, having girded your waist with truth, having put on the breastplate of righteousness, and having shod your feet with the preparation of the gospel of peace; above all, taking the shield of faith with which you will be able to quench all the fiery darts of the wicked one. And take the helmet of salvation, and the sword of the Spirit, which is the word of God; praying always with all prayer and supplication in the Spirit, being watchful to this end with all perseverance and supplication for all the saints.*

> (Ephesians 6:13-18 NKJV)

Within this passage is the correct blueprint for spiritual warfare. Paul, metaphorically, uses the weapons of the Roman soldier to extrapolate on the importance of being ready for battle. Phrases like having your waist girded with truth, feet shod with the preparation of the gospel of peace and the sword of the Spirit help us grasp the importance of not allowing any part of our lives to be exposed to the enemy. Although most preachers and commentators spend great detail on the specific pieces of armor outlined in this passage, it is important to understand that without prayer the weaponry will not help us. We put on this armor by praying always. Prayer is the glue that holds the armor together. Jesus gave us a great example of this when he was tempted by the devil in the wilderness in Matthew 4:4. Our Lord gave us the example of putting on this armor by what He did before encountering the enemy. He prayed and fasted for forty days and forty nights after being baptized in the Spirit in the Jordan River. He was consumed with the presence of God after spending so much time in the Father's presence. When Satan came to Him, he was ready. He used the sword of the Spirit to defeat the enemy in the wilderness. Each time the devil tempted Him, Jesus used the phrase, "It is written" and filled in the blanks from Scripture.

Prayer gives us direction as to what spiritual weapon we will use. We need to pray with confidence and humility. As I was praying for our church to grow and praying against spiritual forces of wickedness, I was praying with confidence but not with humility. I was looking for a fight with the enemy most of the time and I was getting hit because I did it in ignorance. Scripture admonishes us to pray on all occasions and to pray for our brothers and sisters. Satan is real and there are principalities that are over geographic areas. Our job is to pray for the saints and for people on the earth that are bound by the enemy. In fact, Jesus gave us our marching orders, before He ascended into heaven:

> *And He said to them, "Go into all the world and preach the gospel to every creature. He who believes and is baptized will be saved; but he who does not believe will be condemned. And these signs will follow those who believe: In My name they will cast out demons; they will speak with new tongues..."* (Mark 16:15 NKJV)

As we see from Mark 16:15-17, casting out demons is part of fulfilling the great commission. We have been given authority to cast out demons that are on the earth oppressing people. The earth is where we have our dominion. We are not just fulfilling the words of Jesus when we cast our demons, pray for the sick and raise the dead, but we are walking out the original design of humankind—to subdue the earth.

Lastly, Satan is a worthy adversary and need not be feared but respected. We can walk in boldness, knowing that Jesus has won the ultimate victory. The book of Jude warned the early Church, however, not to engage in spiritual warfare incorrectly like the false teachers, especially by reviling Satan:

> *As Sodom and Gomorrah, and the cities around them in a similar manner to these, having given themselves over to sexual immorality and gone after strange flesh, are set forth as an example, suffering the vengeance of eternal fire. Likewise, also these dreamers defile the flesh, reject authority, and speak evil of dignitaries. Yet Michael the archangel, in contending with the devil, when he disputed about the body of Moses, dared not bring against him a reviling accusation, but said, "The Lord rebuke you!" But these speak evil of whatever they do not know; and whatever*

they know naturally, like brute beasts, in these things they corrupt themselves. (Jude 1:7-10 NKJV)

Although Jude goes into great detail to describe the depravity of the false leaders in the passage above, even comparing them to Sodom and Gomorrah and brute beasts, we must be careful not to follow their example to think that we should say slanderous words against high ranking spiritual dignitaries, especially Satan. I mentioned previously that I adopted an unhealthy mindset about spiritual warfare from a well-known individual that I respected a great deal because of the way this person spoke against the enemy. This person later fell due to sexual immorality. I believe he stumbled because he left himself open to counterattacks because of a lack of respect for Satan's ability to deceive. Notice that Michael the archangel did not revile Satan but relied upon God's authority by simply saying, *"the Lord rebuke you."* The authority that we have is in Christ. The enemy likes to coax us into thinking that we are powerful on our own and that we have somehow joined an elite force of spiritual warfare "Green Berets" that can command regional principalities at will.

Needless to say this attitude is a far from the humility that Jesus walked in while He was on the earth. In the Lord's Prayer, Jesus prayed, *"keep us from the evil one."* (Matthew 6:13 NKJV). Within this petition in the Lord's Prayer is the correct way to deal with Satan. We must deal with him in strength of the Spirit with humility. Jesus modeled how we are to go about spiritual warfare. We are to rely upon the Lord's help to overcome the snares of the evil one. This part of the Lord's Prayer is acknowledging that we cannot overcome the schemes of the enemy on our own. We need the Holy Spirit to empower us and give us the grace to stand against the evil one.

Should We Ever Pray Against a Principality?

Though I caution people to follow our Lord's example, to take my advice and the admonition of the late John Paul Jackson as to proper engagement against principalities, I am of the belief that we must war against principalities only when we are led into this kind of warfare by the Spirit of God. There has been much confusion about the topic of praying against principalities. There are many who have adopted an extreme position on second heaven warfare that is filled with fear. Some have given much ground to the enemy because they live in constant fear of counterattack from principalities. We must understand that God has not given us a spirit of fear but of power, love and a sound mind (2 Timothy 1:7).

If the Holy Spirit reveals the plan of the enemy by exposing a particular principality in your region and has confirmed that He wants you to war against it, you must be obedient. God has revealed the spirit to you because He wants you to engage in spiritual warfare against it. Rebecca Greenwood, in her book entitled, *Glory Warfare: How the Presence of God Empowers You to Destroy the Works of Darkness* gives a great example of being led by the Holy Spirit to battle a principality.

> Because of my calling to deliverance, prophetic intercession, and strategic warfare prayer, there have been several instances when demonic entities have attempted to intimidate me from advancing. In one such occasion, we were contending against the spirits behind abortion... Wichita, Kansas, housed an abortion clinic run by a doctor who was viewed by the public and self-satisfied as America's most productive abortionist, Dr. George Tiller.

In his lifetime work, he aborted no less than sixty thousand unborn infants. Abortions, including late-term abortions, were the only medical procedures he executed in his practice. I returned in the fall of 2007, which proved to be a divinely appointed and orchestrated spiritual warfare assignment. For months, believers in the state had been aggressively researching and praying that the spiritual root or demonic principality behind the notorious abortion clinic would be exposed. In preparation for our coming prophetic act, we prayed, asking the Lord to disclose the stronghold. At that moment, the Lord remarkably brought back to my memory a dream I had in 1994 in which He revealed to me the demonic spiritual entity lilith. She is cited in Isaiah 34: 14 as the night monster. The Hebrew word is lilim or lilith, whose name means the night monster, night hag, or screeching owl... In the dream the Lord expressly showed me this territorial deity to be one of the principal forces behind death and abortion.[47]

As Rebecca researched this spirit, she discovered that lilith was an ancient deity depicted as a nocturnal great-winged goddess with bird clawed feet.[48] She also discovered that lilith was known as the goddess of death or Hades. After Rebecca shared her revelation with the prayer team, they all came to the conclusion that this was the principality perpetuating death through abortion. They decided to pray in front of the abortion clinic. As they prayed, Rebecca stated that she heard from the Lord and spoke the following words:

---

47 Rebecca Greenwood, *Glory Warfare: How the Presence of God Empowers You to Destroy the Works of Darkness* (Destiny Image: 2018), Kindle Edition 43-44.

48 Ibid., 44.

"Becca, bind the territorial spirit operating behind the killings of this clinic." I declared, "In the name of Jesus I bind the territorial spirit of death. I bind you, lilith, and say you no longer will be able to execute bloodshed of the innocent and unborn from this location!"[49]

After confrontation with the spirit coupled with the consistent prayers of other prayer warriors, Dr. Tiller began to encounter legal issues on his repeated pattern of late term abortions. As Tiller's illegal abortion practices began to be more exposed, the abortion rate in his clinic declined. The clinic eventually closed after the tragic death of Dr. George Tiller on May 31st 2009. Unfortunately, he was shot by an assassin while serving as an usher at his church. Though Rebecca and many other proponents of life were saddened and condemned the violence perpetrated on Tiller, they were also grateful that the "holocaust of babies at the clinic in Wichita ended."[50]

I believe abortions at the clinic in Wichita clinic ended because Rebecca was obedient and followed the leading of the Holy Spirit who revealed the principality affecting the situation in Kansas. She did not become a needless casualty of war because she approached warfare the right way—under the direction of the Holy Spirit and not through presumption.

Spiritual warfare is a reality and we must understand the schemes of the enemy and how he attacks us, particularly as it pertains to standing for revival. It is comparable to the book of Nehemiah and how God sent Nehemiah and the children of Israel to rebuild the walls. Nehemiah received disturbing news from messengers from Judah about the remnant that had escaped the

49 Ibid., 45.
50 Ibid., 47.

captivity of the Babylonians. The walls to the city of Jerusalem were broken down and the gates were burned (Nehemiah 1:2-3). Nehemiah prayed and fasted and was given a leave of absence by King Artaxerxes to go rebuild the wall in Jerusalem. The Lord gave Nehemiah favor and he was authorized by the king to start the work. When Nehemiah began the task of rebuilding, he began to encounter warfare.

> *But when Sanballat the Horonite, Tobiah the Ammonite official, and Geshem the Arab heard of it, they laughed at us and despised us, and said, "What is this thing that you are doing? Will you rebel against the king?"* (Nehemiah 2:19 NKJV)

Although these three enemies continued to threaten and harass Nehemiah throughout his time in Jerusalem, Nehemiah was able to stay focused on the mission that God had given him. The walls were rebuilt under Nehemiah's leadership because he knew that God had his back. We must walk in that same assurance that Nehemiah had. We must take the approach of Nehemiah when we are persecuted and criticized by messengers of Satan.

> *...that Sanballat and Geshem sent to me, saying, "Come, let us meet together among the villages in the plain of Ono." But they thought to do me harm. So I sent messengers to them, saying, "I am doing a great work, so that I cannot come down. Why should the work cease while I leave it and go down to you?"* (Nehemiah 6:2-3 NKJV)

As we courageously contend for revival in our nation, we must realize that we are doing a great work of rebuilding walls that have been torn down but God is with us to raise them up again. We must not give in to fear or "come down" to the enemy's level. God has given us authority over all the power of Satan. No matter what adversary comes our way, you can "rebuild the walls" if you will not sink to your enemy's level by walking in fear but by standing your ground by walking in courage. In the next section of this chapter, I will address an enemy of revival that is responsible for church splits, family divisions, political division, confusion, murder and utter rebellion—the Jezebel spirit. Most churches and church leaders do not realize it, but many of the church splits, sexual immorality and outright rebellion that we encounter in ministry can be traced to a Jezebel spirit that is at work behind the scenes. If the Body of Christ is to experience true revival in our churches, personal lives and in society, she must understand how this spirit is operating in the world today.

Jezebel the Person

Before we discover how this spirit operates in our local churches and the Body of Christ at large, we must first go to Scripture to take a closer look at Jezebel the person. Jezebel's story is found in 1 and 2 Kings. She was the daughter of Ethbaal, king of Tyre/ Sidon and priest of the cult of Baal, a ruthless, sensuous and repulsive false god whose worship involved sexual degradation and immorality. Ahab, king of Israel, married Jezebel and led the nation into Baal worship (1 Kings 16:31).

There are two episodes in the life of Jezebel which characterize her and seem to epitomize the Jezebel spirit. Jezebel had an obsessive passion for domineering and controlling others. When she became queen, she began a relentless campaign to rid Israel of all evidence of worship to the one true God. She ordered the execution of all the prophets of the Lord (1 Kings 18:4, 13) and replaced their altars with those of Baal. Her strongest enemy was Elijah who demanded a contest on Mount Carmel between the powers of Israel's God and the demonic powers of Jezebel and the priests of Baal (1 Kings 18). Whoever was able to answer by fire and consume the sacrifice would be declared the winner heralded as the true God. It really was no contest. The prophets of Baal cried and invoked the name of Baal morning until evening, even to the point of cutting themselves but to no avail (1 Kings 18:27-28). Elijah began to mock them and suggested that perhaps Baal had not responded because he had to take a trip or that perhaps he was relieving himself (1 Kings 18:27). God answered by fire from heaven when Elijah prayed and consumed the sacrifice. Elijah called for the deaths of eight hundred and fifty prophets of Baal. In spite of hearing about the miraculous power of the true God, Jezebel refused to repent and swore by her gods that she would take the life of Elijah. Her stubbornness and pride would eventually lead to her tragic death (2 Kings 9:29-37).

A second example that epitomized the reign of Jezebel involved a man named Naboth who refused to sell his land to Ahab. King Ahab wanted Naboth's land because it was conveniently located next to the palace. Naboth rightly declared that to sell his inheritance would be against the Lord's command (1 Kings 21:3; Leviticus 25:23). After receiving the news of Naboth's decision not to sale his land, Ahab went away sullen and depressed. He lay down on his bed and would not eat. While Ahab sulked and seethed on his bed, Jezebel ridiculed him for his weakness and then promised that she would get him Naboth's vineyard (1 Kings 21:7). She had Naboth framed and had two false witnesses claim that Naboth blasphemed God and the king (1 Kings 21:13). The people then drove Naboth out of the city and stoned him.

Such an unwavering resolve to have one's way, no matter who is destroyed in the process, is typical of the Jezebel spirit.

So notorious was Jezebel's sexual immorality and idol worship that the Lord Jesus himself referred to her in a warning to the church at Thyatira (Revelation 2:18-29). In his warning to the church, Jesus admonished the church at Thyatira that they were allowing a woman in the church to influence them in the same way that Jezebel influenced Israel into idolatry and sexual immorality. Jesus declared to the Thyatirans that she was not to be tolerated. Like Jezebel, this woman refused to repent of her immorality and her false teaching. The Lord Jesus threw her onto a sick bed, alongside those who committed idolatry with her. Tragically, the end of those who submit to a Jezebel spirit is always death and destruction, both in the physical and the spiritual sense. Perhaps the best approach to describe the Jezebel spirit is to say that it typifies anyone who operates in the same manner as Jezebel did, engaging in immorality, idolatry, control, manipulation, false teaching and unrepentant sin. In the next section we will explain how this spirit operates and how it can wreak havoc, particularly in ministries.

Jezebel's Traits and Partners in Crime

The Jezebel spirit is not as powerful as some have made it out to be. The issue with this spirit is that it is crafty and is able to tear down ministries because it has several partners in crime. One such face of Jezebel is her partner, Ahab. In order for a Jezebel spirit to succeed in tearing down a church, ministry or business, it must have cooperation from Ahab. As we mentioned previously in the last section, Ahab was a weak king of Israel who, along with his wife Jezebel, led the children of Israel into Baal worship.

A Jezebel spirit can flourish in a setting where you have passive men in the church or in a home with men who never demonstrate any leadership or who abdicate their authority by giving power of attorney in all spiritual matters to their wives. I have seen this up close and it is not a pretty picture. One example that stands out is a woman that we will give the name "Sister Applesauce."

When my wife and I first arrived to pastor the church, we began to take note of Sister Applesauce. At first she seemed very pious and focused on prayer and holy living. She would cry at the drop of a hat anytime there was corporate prayer or if she was testifying about something. She loved to cook and serve as she opened up her home to visiting missionaries, and other couples. We began, however, to notice things that concerned us about her. She would try to correct me as the pastor and also do the same thing in the women's Bible Study group. I also began to see her having issues with my elders when she tried to correct them as well. I interviewed one of my elders and he informed me that she had been doing this for quite some time before I arrived. Most of the time people would try to placate her by avoiding confrontation with her. Two of the primary activities that a person with a Jezebel spirit engages in within a local church are correction and false teaching. A person under the guidance of this spirit must correct people, especially the leaders. In order to sustain or grow in power, they need a person with an Ahab spirit that will cooperate with them. In the biblical story, Jezebel was able to accomplish much evil in Israel because she worked with her husband Ahab and was able to wield his power. The Jezebel spirit will do the same thing in the local church but she wants to use pastoral authority. That means that they will work through the pastor of the church to accomplish their goals. The reason why this spirit is so difficult to deal with is that the person is extremely helpful in ministry and they build up emotional capital with many in the church and with the pastoral leadership.

Sister Applesauce was empowered by the pastoral leadership team because she was very helpful and filled a necessary void in the church for service. It was not long before she was inviting the elders and their wives to her house for dinner to discuss changes that she felt needed to be made if only the new young pastor of the church would listen. It is important to understand that people who operate like this are hurting and need our prayers. The purpose of this section is not to promote a witch-hunt to track down people so that we can rid ourselves of them. We want to expose this spirit and deliver the person from being oppressed by them. One of the main issues with Sister Applesauce was that she was in emotional pain because of her family. Her husband struggled with an Ahab spirit and was very passive in spiritual matters. He was a tender-hearted person and a good provider but was constantly withdrawing from his wife. The couple had two sons but they were not involved in the church. She really wanted a good marriage but did not understand that submission was a key component.

Submission is a word that a person with a Jezebel spirit struggles with. After all, submission carries the tone of giving up control and this is completely antithetical to the spirit of Jezebel that wants to rule and not to submit. The Jezebel spirit will give the appearance of submitting to gain favor with pastoral leadership but there will always be a price tag on this kind of cooperation. For instance, Sister Applesauce seemed to have a real heart for prayer. She was one of the few people that I could count on to show up for prayer on time. She was also important to our outreach ministries and was always willing to walk from house to house giving out flyers and willing to pitch in to do whatever was necessary for the mission to go forward. However, each time she would serve in this manner, there was price to pay. On one occasion she criticized the pastor (me) in front of other members of the church in the middle of a community outreach event. She had worked hard as usual that day but undermined the pastor claiming she knew what was best and that others should not listen to the pastor because he really did not know what he was doing. Her behavior that day not only affected the people who came to the outreach, but she caused confusion for one of the members who eventually left the church.

Sister Applesauce and her husband left the church eventually because I would not succumb to her controlling tendencies, sowing discord among brethren and her constant attempts to bring correction to me and to any other person who she could get to listen to her doctrine. After she left the church, I was able to interview a fellow pastor who knew about her from years ago. He informed me that she had been in several churches before attending our church doing similar things to pastors. She would even take advantage of passive pastors who were afraid to confront her by taking over the entire service with a long testimony that made it nearly impossible for the pastor to even preach in the morning service.

A Python Spirit

A trait that I have seen in the Jezebel spirit is that it acts like a python snake. In order to eat its prey, the python snake constricts and squeezes its prey until there is no more breath left in its victim. This makes it easier for the snake to swallow its victim whole. One of the things that we must be aware of when this face of Jezebel is at work is that you literally feel like something is squeezing the life out of you. It will make you want to quit before a Holy Spirit outpouring. The squeezing from this face of Jezebel may come in the form of nagging sicknesses, lack of financial resources, exiting church members or a compilation of these happening all at the same time.

A few years ago, the Holy Spirit gave me a dream to give me insight into the way this spirit works within the Body of Christ. One night I was dreaming that I was lying down in what appeared to be a watery grave. I was amazed at how much peace that I felt while I was lying in this awful place. If I was in the natural, it would have been absolutely terrifying. As I was lying there, I began to say in my mind, "I know that I am going to be raised." This went on for several minutes. Then suddenly I decided to get up. As I looked down at my feet, I saw dead fish all over the place. I then looked into an old dusty mirror and saw what appeared to be leeches on parts of my face. I pulled them off and then noticed something to my right that was even more startling. To my right was a huge python snake that appeared to be sleeping. I knew instantly that this snake was responsible for all the dead fish in this place and was overseeing everything. I began to look for something to kill the snake before it woke up. As the snake was starting to wake up, the dream ended. When I woke from the dream, I began to pray and the Holy Spirit began to give me the interpretation. The dead fish represented people in the Body of Christ that had succumbed to this spirit. Their spiritual lives had become lifeless just like the dead fish in the watery grave. The enemy had squeezed the life right out of them by suffocating them with financial pressure, family issues and mental torment. Many of the believers in this predicament had stopped attending church because they became consumed with their work schedules instead of worshipping in the house of God.

I remember one lady in our congregation that definitely fitted this description. She became part of the church and was being blessed. The enemy began to put pressure on her financially and she began to panic. She began to work on Sundays and stopped showing up for the Wednesday service. Every couple of months I would run into her at the local grocery store. I would just encourage her and tell her that the enemy was trying to take life out of her. Every time we connected, she would affirm what I was saying but had become so weak that she would not even attend a service when she was available. She no longer attends church and has lost her spiritual fervor.

The python spirit was not only at work in the pews but it was squeezing the life right out of us. The enemy brought tremendous financial stress on us due to lack of support from people at the church who tried to control us because we wanted the manifest presence of God more than the favor of man. My dream about this huge reptile was also a self-inventory dream. It represented my current condition in ministry. My wife and I both felt like the problems in the church had taken away much of our joy and peace. The dream gave me strength because I knew the Holy Spirit was showing me what the enemy was doing. Despite Satan's attacks, I knew that I was going to be raised back to life. Yet, there was still another trait of Jezebel that the Holy Spirit wanted to teach me about.

Absalom

In Scripture, Absalom was the handsome son of King David who turned against his father and stole the hearts of the people of Israel in an attempt to murder his father and gain the throne (2 Samuel 15:4-6). Absalom would sit at the gate of the city, meeting with anyone who had a grievance to gain their trust and favor. He persuaded the people that his judgment on matters pertaining to them would be more just than his father David. If the Jezebel spirit is active in your ministry, some of the men will take on the traits of Absalom. In order to detect this spirit, we need to understand its characteristics.

One trait of an Absalom is that the person usually has a close relationship or has access to the leader. In David's case, Absalom happened to be his son. In a church or ministry setting, Absalom can be a spiritual son (which can be devastating to a pastor). In our case, it was an elder that had access and influence with me as the senior pastor. When we first arrived, the elder was helpful to us. He actually helped us move into our new house. We started having problems with him when I began to hear that people in the congregation were coming to this particular elder with complaints about me and the changes we were making at the church. The elder began to entertain more grievances about me and would consistently represent the old wineskin system in the church. This is yet another trait of the Absalom spirit. They will always stand as the go-between or political representative of the people in the congregation. In this manner, he was acting like David's son Absalom who had stolen the hearts of the men of Israel by promising that he would deliver justice to their causes.

I tried to intervene before the situation escalated by confronting this brother in love. I shared my concerns with him about the potential for problems if he continued representing the people in this particular fashion. At first he seemed to receive my gentle correction but it was not before long that I came to hear about the secret meetings he was having with influential members of the church. Because he was in leadership at the church, this elder, along with his wife, began to spearhead a group of people who informed me that I was leading the church in the wrong direction. Any changes that my wife and I wanted to make would always be subject to tight scrutiny.

The situation with this elder came to a head when a disgruntled member of the church decided that she wanted to set up a meeting with my wife, the elder and yours truly about a matter concerning the music ministry. The dissatisfied member had already communicated with the elder before the meeting so it felt like we were being set up. At the meeting, the lady began to accuse my wife of being harsh and uncaring with members of the worship team. The accusations were unfounded but the elder was in full support of the woman and did not really give any credence to my wife's side of the story. Although the meeting ended amicably, I knew that the "writing was on the wall" and that the elder could not continue in this capacity for much longer.

I began to really seek the Lord about the situation because the elder already had a great deal of influence in the church because he had been there for over twenty years. The best way to approach an Absalom is to first soak everything in prayer. I was praying for two things—either change the heart of this man or remove him God's way. I could see some good traits in him but also saw things that were conniving and controlling. The second thing that you have to do in dealing with this kind of spirit acting in a person is to humble yourself. In the story of David and Absalom, upon hearing the news that Absalom wanted to take his (David) life and take the kingdom by force, David fled to the Mount of Olives weeping, barefoot and with his head covered (2 Samuel 15:30 NKJV). It is important to underscore here that at the center of everything is pride. This face of Jezebel will not admit if they are wrong. The wrong way to approach them is in anger or to approach them with demanding their respect for your position. Although you may be tempted to remind them that you are the one that God has chosen to lead this church into the move of God that it desperately needs, you will be playing right into the enemy's hands because you would no longer be operating like Jesus in humility. Even though Jesus was equal to God, He did not try to cling to his position but He humbled himself (Philippians 2:5). The person being influenced by the Absalom spirit will try to provoke you into defending yourself and getting into pride. The victory will be accomplished as we submit to the Holy Spirit in love.

Another step in dealing with this spirit is that you have to be specific in praying for the person that is being influenced. As I mentioned previously, I prayed for the elder and his wife. I prayed that God would work in his heart. I also prayed that if it was not the Lord's will that the man stay with us in the fellowship, please remove him. In Scripture, we observe David praying a similar prayer in the case of Absalom. Ahithophel had served previously as David's counselor, but had decided to side with Absalom during the hostile takeover of the kingdom. Here we observe David's prayer regarding the situation: Then someone told David, saying, *"Ahithophel is among the conspirators with Absalom." And David said, "O LORD, I pray, turn the counsel of Ahithophel into foolishness!"* (2 Samuel 15:31 NKJV). Notice in this short prayer that David went after the power behind the throne. Ahithophel knew David's strategies well because he counseled him many times. He was conspiring against the true king of Israel with a self-appointed king and false ruler. We must remember that we wrestle not against flesh and blood but against principalities, powers, rulers of darkness and spiritual wickedness in high places (Ephesians 6:12). Our prayers must be directed against the demonic spirit that is influencing the person.

After prayer, we can expect the Lord to give us a strategy for our particular situation. David not only prayed that God would turn Ahithophel's counsel into foolishness but he instituted a strategy to ensure that Absalom would think twice about following Ahithophel's advice. David sent Hushai, the king's counselor, as a spy to infiltrate the enemy and thwart Absalom's plans.

> *Now it happened when David had come to the top of the mountain, where he worshiped God -- there was Hushai the Archite coming to meet him with his robe torn and dust on his head. David said to him, "If you go on with me, then you will become a burden to me. But if you return to the city, and say to Absalom, 'I will be your servant, O king; as I was your father's servant previously, so I will now also be your servant,' then you may defeat the counsel of Ahithophel for me.* (2 Samuel 15:32-34 NKJV)

It was an emotional time for David and all those who supported him. He could not let his feelings get in the way of good judgement. Hushai was more valuable to the king by keeping his ear ready to receive information about the plans of Absalom. David's plan would work to perfection when Hushai followed the king's wishes by going back and serving in Absalom's administration. Hushai defeated Ahithophel's good advice when he convinced Absalom to gather the entire army to defeat David instead of going with Ahithophel's plan to destroy David with only twelve thousand men (2 Samuel 17:1-14). The result for heeding the advice of David's spy was disastrous for Absalom as he was killed later in the battle. Ahithophel also decided to take his own life because his advice was not followed.

Similar to David, the Lord also gave me a plan after prayer. The biggest part of the plan centered on patience. I had to display perseverance because the enemy kept trying to provoke me into a war of words with this man. I had to wait for the Lord to work things out. Finally, one day the elder sent an email to me that was divisive in tone. I forwarded the email to my District Superintendent (DS). I had made my DS aware of the situation months ago and now things had escalated. It is important to get support from those that you trust and that are in authority.

When my District Superintendent saw the email, he became convinced that the elder had disqualified himself from leadership. This would eventually lead to a meeting between me, the DS and the elder. The meeting was not a blame session but it was designed to follow the Bible's protocol for dealing with conflict as set forth in Matthew's gospel.

> "Moreover if your brother sins against you, go and tell him his fault between you and him alone. If he hears you, you have gained your brother. But if he will not hear, take with you one or two more, that 'by the mouth of two or three witnesses every word may be established.' And if he refuses to hear them, tell it to the church. But if he refuses even to hear the church, let him be to you like a heathen and a tax collector. (Matthew 18:15-17 NKJV)

In the meeting the District Superintendent gave his support to me and my wife. He did not try to correct or chastise the elder but tried to make him understand that the changes that I was trying to institute in the church were necessary in order to bring the church back to health. The elder did not see it that way. His primary complaint was in the area of worship but instead of talking to us openly about his differences of opinion, he began to create strife and dissension behind my back. Needless to say, after this meeting, he called me a week later to inform me that he and his wife would not be attending the church any longer.

I was relieved but also knew that he was one of my best tithers and that he had relationships with other people in the church. Eventually, the people who supported him left as well. You must understand that there may be repercussions when you display courage and confront an individual who is being influenced by a Jezebel spirit. If the person does not repent, they have the potential to take others with them due to the emotional capital they have built up during their time in the ministry. In this particular instance, the elder had almost twenty years in the church. It was difficult because the church was small with limited resources to begin with. We had to trust in the Lord as our provider. I believe one of the main reasons why churches do not experience the move of God is that leaders are afraid to lose people and their financial resources. They want to keep the status quo even though the Holy Spirit is trying to alter the status quo. We must realize that the boat that we are trying not to rock is eventually going to sink anyway if we do not confront the real enemy that is influencing the people and hindering a move of God. If you do not confront Absaloms, they will stay and gain more influence and take more people with them when they decide to leave. If this happens, the results are usually devastating to a church or ministry. The pastor will be left trying to pick up the pieces in a church that has been gutted by another face of Jezebel.

Leviathan

The last spirit partner of Jezebel that you must beware of is Leviathan. The word Leviathan appears first in the Old Testament in the book of Job chapter 3 verse 8 when Job was cursing the day he was born. The term Leviathan has been debated for years in scholarly circles as to what the word really means. Some think that Leviathan was actually a real sea creature that had become extinct, while others assert that the word was spiritual in nature pertaining to the "twisted" nature of the devil. For the sake of this current work, I want to concentrate primarily on the spiritual meaning of Leviathan.

As a pastor, I have had many close encounters with the face of Leviathan in ministry. When this spirit is in operation, the person will constantly twist or spin their version of the "truth" in most situations. Confusion will also be present because they may hear something entirely different from what is being communicated by the leader. There are those who have this spirit and have no clue that they are even victims. Conversely, there are those who are willing participants and in league with this spirit. They are what our Lord describes as tares sown among the wheat (Matthew 13:24-30). These people have been sent by the enemy to delay or in some cases stop the move of God from occurring by practicing witchcraft.

In the case of the unsuspecting victims of Leviathan, I have found that they have truly received Jesus as their Lord and Savior. They are simply unaware of generational curses in their families' histories affecting their behavior. One example I recall is a woman that I will give the name "Greta." Greta came to our church one evening for a private deliverance session because she was being tormented by the demonic. We actually have a deliverance team at our church and we partner with a wonderful deliverance minister who is a good friend of mine. Deliverance is another term for the biblical practice of casting out demons. Greta was a successful businesswoman who attended a megachurch in a nearby city forty minutes away from us.

Greta informed us that she was a lay leader at her church and that she was also involved in intercessory ministry. She began to inform us of her pastor's shortcomings and began to explain how God had given her a vision for the church but the pastor was just not on board. As we listened to her it became apparent that she had fallen victim to a Jezebel spirit. She could only find fault with her leaders and never took any responsibility for her own shortcomings. As we tried to help her understand what she was doing, we also noticed that she began to refute and twist our words, alerting us that Leviathan was also present. Before the session ended, we led her in a prayer of repentance and cast out several demons.

Greta's story is important because she represents a growing number of sincere believers that are unwilling vessels that the enemy is using to spread division within the Body of Christ. Whether the spirit of Jezebel is accompanied by an Ahab partner, Leviathan comrade or has Python or Absalom traits, we must realize that it is an enemy to the move of the Holy Spirit. Many churches and ministries are being hindered because many pastors, leaders and other believers have been intimidated by this spirit just like the prophet Elijah who ran away from Jezebel after she threatened to take his life. We must remember the words of Jesus to the church of Thyatira who gave the command to not tolerate her any longer.

> *"Nevertheless I have a few things against you, because you allow that woman Jezebel, who calls herself a prophetess, to teach and seduce My servants to commit sexual immorality and eat things sacrificed to idols. And I gave her time to repent of her sexual immorality, and she did not repent. Indeed, I will cast her into a sickbed, and those who commit adultery with her into great tribulation, unless they repent of their deeds. I will kill her children with death, and all the churches shall know that I am He who searches the minds and hearts. And I will give to each one of you according to your works."* (Revelation 2:20–23 NKJV)

It takes courage to stand your ground in the midst of spiritual warfare and the attacks of Jezebel. Sometimes we can get so caught up with the wonderful prophetic words about the Glory and the coming move of God that we forget that the enemy is not just going to lie down while we bask in the presence of God. He wants to sabotage things by getting us distracted with political quarrels, division in the church, fear, apathy, spiritual laziness and sin. Like the early apostles we must demonstrate boldness and perseverance in the midst of intimidation and realize that persecution often comes with the move of God. Lord, give us courageous hearts!

A Final Word

Like so many other prophetic voices in our nation, I too believe that we are on the precipice of the greatest move of God that we have ever seen. Even now, in some parts of the world we are starting to experience the glory of the Lord. It's an exciting time to be alive. The Lord put this book on my heart for two reasons.

Firstly, I wanted to encourage my brothers and sisters in the Body of Christ who have been actively contending for revival for years and have become a bit discouraged. Many of you have been through the fire and back again. After reading the pages of this book, I believe that you realize now that your heart was being prepared by the Lord and your breakthrough is right around the corner. You have been broken, you are hungry for God, you have stayed prayerful, you have been persistent, thankful and have demonstrated courage in the midst of seemingly impossible circumstances.

Secondly, I wanted to encourage those of you who have become distracted and have lost some of your passion to use this book as a litmus test. The six heart indicators that I have covered are things that I have observed and experienced in my twenty-five plus years in ministry. As I mentioned previously, these six heart elements have not been included to be formulaic but are indicative of the way that I have observed the Lord work in the lives of many who have experienced personal and corporate revival. May they serve as encouraging signs to spur you on to press into God more so that you experience all that God has for you!

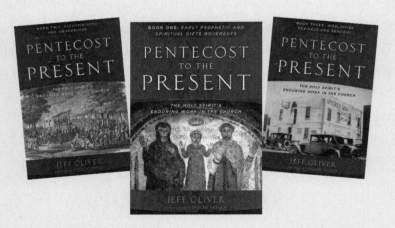

I BELIEVE IN MIRACLES
Kathryn Kuhlman

Your faith will be inspired as you read how Carey Reams threw his crutches away, how George Orr's sight was restored, and how Elizabeth Gethin's heart condition was healed—plus the testimonies of eighteen others healed by God.

Through these incredible testimonies, Kathryn Kuhlman continues to demonstrate God's compassion and awesome power, as she did throughout her life. Discover for yourself the keys to new life and victory through the miracle work and ministry of one of God's great servants.

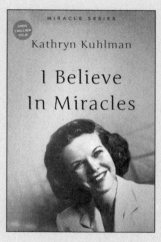

ISBN: 978-0-88270-657-3

BRIDGE
LOGOS

GOD CAN DO IT AGAIN
Kathryn Kuhlman

Kathryn Kuhlman has brought together the first-person stories of several people who have been cured of ills ranging from multiple sclerosis to spiritual emptiness. Each page radiates with Miss Kuhlman's love for God and His love for all mankind.

Read these amazing testimonies wrought by God's extraordinary servant, and know that God can do it again for you! This is a book that will inspire your faith for healing, and the faith of anyone you give it to.

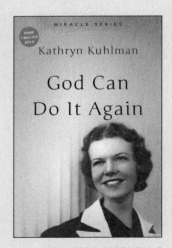

ISBN: 978-0-88270-710-5

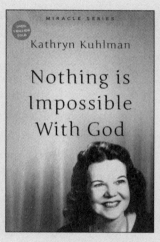

EVIDENCE BIBLE
Ray Comfort

Apologetic answers to over 200 questions, thousands of comments, and over 130 informative articles will help you better comprehend and share the Christian faith.

ISBN: 9780882705255

SCIENTIFIC FACTS IN THE BIBLE
Ray Comfort

Most people, even Christians, don't know that the Bible contains a wealth of incredible scientific, medical, and prophetic facts. That being so, the implications are mind boggling.

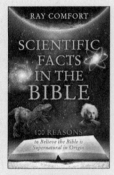

ISBN: 9780882708799

HOW TO KNOW GOD EXISTS
Ray Comfort

Does God exist, or does He not? In this compelling book, Ray Comfort argues the case with simple logic and common sense. This book will convince you that belief in God is reasonable and rational—a matter of fact and not faith.

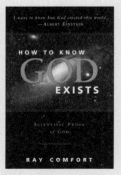

ISBN: 9780882704326

SCHOOL OF BIBLICAL EVANGELISM
Ray Comfort & Kirk Cameron

This comprehensive study offers 101 lessons on thought-provoking topics including basic Christian doctrines, cults and other religions, creation/evolution, and more. Learn how to share your faith simply, effectively, and biblically... the way Jesus did.

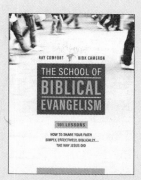

ISBN: 9780882709680

WAY OF THE MASTER STUDENT EDITION
Ray Comfort & Allen Atzbi

Youth today are being inundated with opposing messages, and desperately need to hear the truth of the gospel. How can you reach them? Sharing the good news is much easier than you think... by using some timeless principles.

ISBN: 9781610364737

BRIDGE LOGOS

FOR A COMPLETE LIST OF BOOKS, TRACTS, AND VIDEOS BY RAY COMFORT, SEE

LIVINGWATERS.COM

GOD'S GENERALS FOR KIDS (SERIES)
Roberts Liardon & Olly Goldenberg

This series has been growing in popularity and it focusses on the lives and teachings of great Christian leaders from times past. These books are written for children between the ages of eight and twelve. Newly released and enhanced, each book now includes an updated study section with cross curricular themes, suitable for home schooling groups. Kathryn Kuhlman (Vol. 1), and Smith Wigglesworth (Vol. 2) begin the series. Other Generals to be released over the coming 12 months are: John Alexander Dowie, Maria Woodworth-Etter, Evan Roberts, Charles Parham, William Seymour, John G. Lake, Aimee Semple McPherson, William Branham, Jack Coe and A.A. Allen.